A Hobbyists Guide to Turning and DIY
Ideas for inspiration

A Hobbyists Guide to Turning and DIY - Ideas for inspiration

A Hobbyists Guide to Turning and DIY
Ideas for inspiration

Kenneth B. Moore

Publisher Kenneth B. Moore

Year of Publication 2015

A Hobbyists Guide to Turning and DIY - Ideas for inspiration

Copyright © 2014 by Kenneth B. Moore

All rights reserved. This book or any portion thereof may not be reproduced or used in any manner whatsoever without the express written permission of the publisher except for the use of brief quotations in a book review or scholarly journal.

First Printing: 2015

ISBN – 13: 978-1514718513

www.handycrafted.net

Dedication

To wife Sarah, and children, Lauren Amy and Thomas.

You are the most important people in my life.

Without your patience and understanding

I would have never have put pen to paper

Thank you and love always.

A Hobbyists Guide to Turning and DIY - Ideas for inspiration

Contents

Preface	1
Introduction	3
1: Basic Introduction to Wood Turning for Fun, for Gifts, for Safety	5
2: Making a Pen is Easy and Fun	13
3: Wooden Christmas Bauble Tree Ornament	19
4: Wooden Cube in a sphere Christmas Bauble Tree Ornament	23
5: Wooden Christmas Carousel Ornament	25
6: A Wand for Harry Potter - Magic	31
7: Spinning Top and Helicopter	37
8: Hand Turned Tea light or Eggcup	43
9: Recycling paper to make seed pots	47
10: DIY Drum Sander	51
11: Up from the Ashes a Mantel Piece renovation	53
12: Door Trimming Jig	61
13: A Motor Bike - What a Rocking Ride	63
14: Hobby Horse	71
15: Trailer Trolley	77
16: An old fashioned bogie kart	83
About the Author	87

Preface

First let me say thank you for taking the time to read this book, it's on a subject that I love – the creation of objects that are sometimes useful, sometimes attractive, but always fun to make.

Woodwork and D.I.Y. are incredibly big and sometimes complex subjects and I will not be dealing with all forms only the one that I find great fun… 'Wood' Turning. The question marks are there because wood is not the only material available to you for this hobby, others include

Wood…… (obviously)

Resins.. You might have heard about Corian, (this just one brand) another is called Velstone

Deer antler and other forms of horn e.g. buffalo (as long as it's not endangered and you get from reputable source)

Polyurethane resins…. These you mix yourself and cast your own blanks

Just a few I'm sure there are others.

I've included a number of projects in this book and one thing to keep in mind is that every material will have its own working properties so have a bit of a practice before you start your creations using a bit of scrap or you will find as I have that the project will soon become scrap itself.

I am not claiming to be an expert this book contains projects that I have created using skills and practices that I have developed – it will not teach you how to use a lathe, which comes with practice and patience.

Here are a few of the pens I've created using various pattern ideas and three different materials: Velstone resin, Buffalo Horn and a wood called Purple Heart.

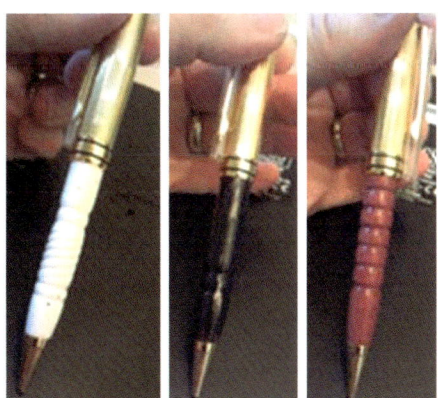

The objects you can make are limited only by your imaginatio9ns - so have fun.

A Hobbyists Guide to Turning and DIY - Ideas for inspiration

Introduction

Hello and thank you for taking the time to consider this book. It is my first, so please excuse any inconsistencies with other books on the subject you may have read.

The book is intended to document projects in wood working that I have crated over a number of years. I have had great fun working of all of my projects and the contents of the following pages contain guides, and instructions, but most of all ideas. Ideas are where all of the instructions started. Ideas for pens, for tools and for toys. Keep in mind when looking through the pages that these are my ideas and if you decide to have a go at recreating one you will add your own, so the final product will always be unique and yours.

I have included a section with some basic safety, but no such content can cover everything, so take it as a starting point and make sure that you read, understand and follow all of the instructions and safety guidance that comes with your tools.

There are 15 chapters in this book, 14 of which are projects for you to read and hopefully get inspiration from, I've mentioned that I had fun creating them and I hope you have fun also.

A Hobbyists Guide to Turning and DIY - Ideas for inspiration

1: Basic Introduction to Wood Turning for Fun, for Gifts, for Safety

Safety

There are a number of safety issues related to having fun in a workshop.

Housekeeping

Turning wood, or any other material creates a lot of debris very quickly, controlling this will help to prevent workshop accidents, slips and trips etc. as well as reducing the levels of combustible materials in the area. For this I have an old vacuum and a brush

Dust

The dust created during your hobby is dangerous to you directly. Breathing it in can affect your lungs, so it is important to protect yourself against its effects, a simple dust extractor is a must and should be used for all activities, I also have a Trend face visor which is battery powered and filters the air being fed to the visor. The visor also gives a level of protection from flying objects as you work the material.

Sharps

Watch your fingers, by its nature working with a lathe means that you will be handling chisels which have to be kept sharp, not only so you shape the materials, but also for your safety. A blunt tool can dig in and put you at risk. So handle and store them with care. And keep them sharp before during and after use

For storage of my chisels I have an MDF board on the wall to which is attached an number of battery clips to hold all of the tools I need, it also has pins to hold other related tools e.g. Lathe jaws.

The lathe is not the only source of cuts others include drills and band saws both of which have fast moving cutting edges with which there is a simple rule. Keep your fingers clear and your eyes open.

Collisions

As mentioned fast moving tools can hurt you without due care. Some injures will result in minor bumps and bruises from glancing blows. A more serious injury will come from you losing concentration while actually working with the lathe. It's incredibly easy to get your fingers, hand trapped between the tools rest and the rotating work piece, especially if your finishing a piece. One such trap can come from losing control of the material you are using to sand your project, which then gets pulled onto and around the spinning work piece and if your not quick enough in letting go your fingers too will get wrapped around your project.

Guides for finishing and turning in general

1. Use the tool rest - keep your hands behind it when the lathe is operating.
2. Never use fabric for application of polish / wax it can snag and pull your hand in.
3. Long hair.... Tie it back and don't reach to the floor while the lathe is spinning.
4. Posture........ It's important to be comfortable while working, make sure the tools are at an appropriate height for you.. This might be a case of trial and error, just take your time.
5. Noise...... Wear ear defenders – you could be working for long periods and some tools can get noisy.
6. Eyes - you are only born with two and they don't grow back. Make sure you use safety specs or more preferably a full face visor.

Things that Spin

All of the tools you use move in one way or another, either under power or by you, make sure to follow manufacturer's instructions at all times. Also you can help protect yourself from these by ensuring that the lighting around your projects is sufficient. And install a light over your lathe to directly illuminate the working area – Parts that are rotating quickly in poor lighting look stationary and it's easy to be fooled into touching them. The light used should be an incandescent bulb not a fluorescent tube.

Vapours

You will at some point be using glues, waxes and polish on you projects most of which will give off some form of vapour, flammable or otherwise. It's important to wear some form of mask especially if you are working for long periods.

It's OK having good ventilation; however exposure can be cumulative so remember to take breaks away from the workshop.

Dermatitis

Not only is dust an inhalation issue, it's also combustible and an irritant. This can be an issue and you would think that using gloves is required. Ordinarily yes, but only for work away from the lathe. Use gloves on the lathe at your own risk as it increases the risk of being pulled into the spinning work. Instead use a thicker bit of tissue to apply the polish etc. to the spinning project.

Turning differing materials

Turning is great fun and using good quality materials will help with this:

Soft Wood	Open grain. Easy to turn, but produces more fibrous particles rather than clean shavings
Hard Wood	Close grain.. Produces clean shavings. However a lot of hard woods get that way from the closeness of the grain as well as a high resin content. While the clean shavings will help keep the dust down the resin will kill the edge on your tool meaning more frequent sharpening is required.
Self-cast resins	greater for pens, but if you catch it while turning it can splinter. Not so bad unless you are close to finishing. I have had a number of pens ruined by this. The important part of this is what I tell my son; "the best thing about having to start over...is.. And he replies... The chance to improve... "He's 9 and gets it.
Corian	This is a propitiatory material used for kitchen work tops and is really great to turn, it works well gives little in the way of catches and chips. Another trade name is Velstone.

Things to watch out for in materials are its natural flaws, e.g. wood (Knots, Cracks / Splits). A lot of flaws can be fixed an need not stop you from using the material. First decide if you like the flaw, if not pick a different piece. If you do then use it, but before you start to turn it find a way to stabilize the fault. Using superglue on cracks or knots is a great method for wood. Let the glue set and then take small cuts ensuring that you keep your tools sharp at all times. Eventually the fault may reappear as you remove more material – just repeat the stabilization by adding more glue.Take care when changing between materials ....everyone has its own characteristics. For example:

- Self-cast resins Solid and can shatter

Corian - Solid, will catch to start with, but once the blank is rounded off will turn very smoothly

Hard woods- Nice shavings lower dust than soft wood

Soft woods - Very easy to turn, lots of fibre dust.

When you get used to soft wood then switch to hard it's easy to catch the spinning material. This can jar you a bit. Don't worry when this happens just try again taking small cuts with sharp tools.

Tools to start turning

The tools are the easy bit.

To start wood turning all you really need is the lathe (with its associated parts ...see individual manufacturers) and a set of good chisels. Don't use them out of the box, while they will have an edge on them they will not be sharp enough to work with, so sharpen them first.

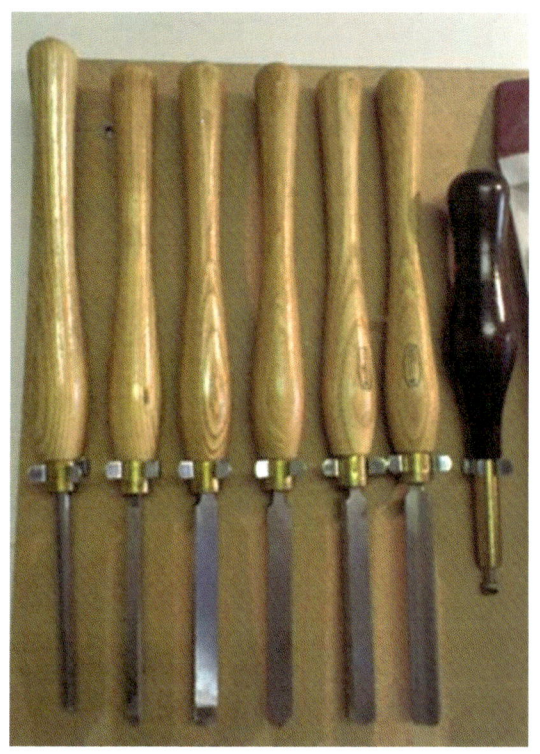

For basic turning the chisels will suffice, but as you improve you will need some more specialized accessories.

For turning pens a Mandrel is a must, a barrel trimming tool is useful for a lot of materials, but not all.

Also for pens – mostly the acrylic types you will find a polishing / buffing wheel useful, and then if you want to get fancy, adding spirals and texture to your designs then tools like the Robert Sorby Micro Spiralling tools is a great addition.

Tools for preparation

Apart from the lathe and chisels, other tools you could find useful for your hobby are:

Pillar drill.... A bench mounted one is sufficient

A selection of drill bits

An orbital sander.... Really a nice to have.

Band saw..... Very useful

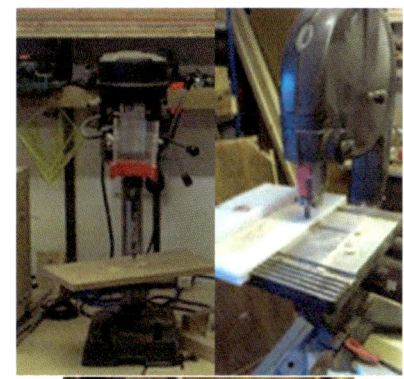

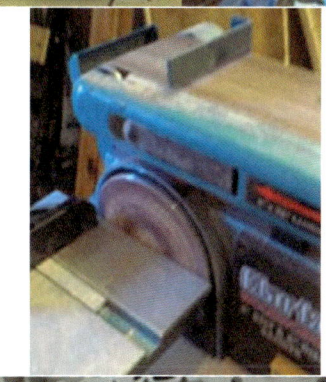

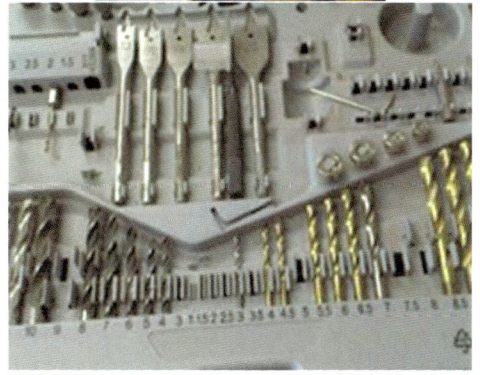

Finishing Your Project

There are a few ways to finish a project one of which is to leave it rough, or you could smooth it by:

Cutting

You can get an almost finished piece on a lathe by ensuring the sharpness of your tools and by practicing. If you get it right you may not even need to sand.

Sanding

Buy a range a sanding grits and work from the course at to finest. The starting grit will depend on how well you turn the piece. When you get to the thinner grits you can also add materials like friction polish or wood wax 22 as you sand to ensure smooth finish.

Burnishing

The shavings you make during turning are not completely wasted. Grab a hand full and use them on the rotating piece, the shavings will polish the wood by friction (simple, cheap and easy)

Super Glue Coat

For pens I sometimes apply super glue to wood pen barrels and polish using pen pads, the combination gives a fantastic finish if you get it right.

Projects Summary

There are a number of projects to follow, here is a quick summary

Decorations

Wooden Cube in a sphere Bauble Ornament, or a Christmas Tree decoration.

A Carousel for Christmas – mixture of snowmen and trees suspended on a roundabout adding motion to decoration a great centre piece.

Pens

Pen making can be both easy and fun there's a simple guide on how to start.

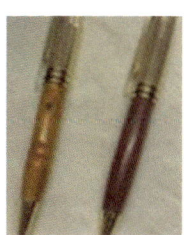

Toys

From Spinning tops and helicopters to magic wands good enough for Harry Potter. These projects demonstrate the use moving parts as well as differing materials in the same design.

Utensils

For the house a hand turned Tea Light or Eggcup you decide and for the garden, recycle your old paper by using this device to make seed pots for your garden plants.

2: Making a Pen is Easy and Fun

I've been turning pens for some time they are great fun to make and the finished items can be attractive, useful and very saleable.

There is a huge range of styles for you to try, and while you can make them from scratch as stick pens (turning the whole pen and simply inserting the refill), the majority come as a kit of basing parts generally consisting of all of the metal parts as well as the refill to complete a full pen, some will also include design patterns and precast blanks for specific effects. What you bring to the party is your skill and imagination when turning your prepared pen blank.

The images above are a few of the pens I have created. These are all made from two sections (top and bottom), however for this guide I have decided to use a simpler set with a metal top and a single turned section. The reason being that the process for turning a single section pen is the same as that for one with two parts, you just have to repeat it twice to get both upper and lower sections.

As mentioned I created all of the pens here, they are made from a variety of materials for a range of pens kit styles, from slim-line twist pen to push pencil and American Flat top push pen. Using materials including Wood (Zebra wood, Paduk, Ebony, Maple, Purple Heart), Resins (Imitation Ivory, Velstone, Hand poured resin on a gold string base).

Everyone works their own way, but I try not to design the pen from the start, finding it more fun to see what develops as you turn the material and feel that the important part is to have fun and enjoy yourself. The more you do then, for me, the better the end product.

Pen kits generally come with some form of diagram; this will tell you how to put all of the parts together. It's a good idea at this point to lay out all the parts to make sure that you have everything required.

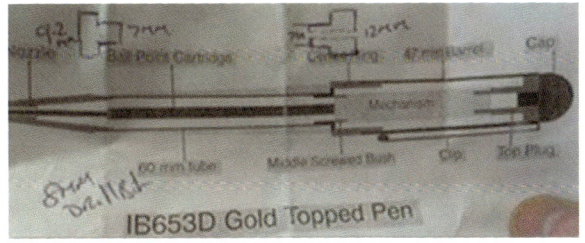

.

IMPORTANT

For most kits at this point do not put any bits together you might not be able to separate them. However for the purpose of this guide the top of the pen is all metal, constructing this part did not cause a problem

BUSHINGS

These are small pieces of metal designed to fit onto a pen mandrel at either end of your pen blank, giving you a static point to which you can reduce your material which then forms the joint between the turned blank and the rest of the pen kit. This particular kit was from discontinued stock, meaning that bushings were not available. In the absence of bushings you will need to either turn by measurement (repeated cutting, stopping and measuring until you get to the dimensions needed), or make your own, I chose to make the bushings.

Brass is a good material for ease, it is soft enough to allow for turning on your wood lathe. Firstly – measure the external diameter of a spare brass pen tube from a slim-line kit. Drilled a hole through the gas fitting the same diameter as the spare brass tube. Then glue the pen tube inside of the gas fitting using epoxy resin. Using callipers measure the parts of the pen kit that will form the joints with the finished pen blank. Also measure the internal diameter of the brass tube to be used in the actual kit being made.

Attach your gas fitting onto a pen mandrel and install that onto you lathe. Turn the brass fitting, using the measurement's you have just taken to make the bushings needed. Take care to stop and measure regularly as they will need to insert into the pen blank to centre it during turning.

  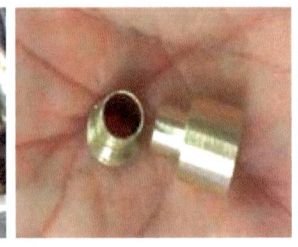 

Blank preparation - drilling

Next step is to prepare the pen blank, start by selecting your wood / material of choice, for this pen I am using a wood called Purple Heart and Maple - two woods as I would be making two pens). Now cut a length that is just longer than the brass tube for the pen blank, mark the centre of the long axis of the piece of wood and drill a hole all the way through using a clamp to safely hold the wood while drilling. Once drilled confirm that the tube fits the hole.

From the pictures you can see that this was done off of the lathe, however more recently I have started to round off the blank on the lathe and then while still in the lathe use it to centre drill the blank – this is more stable and gives a more snug fit for the brass tube.

Blank preparation

Gluing up

Now mix up your epoxy resin (Equal lengths of resin and hardener) place some of the mixture on the external of the brass tube and insert it into the pre-drilled wood, rotate the tube as you insert it and ensure that the glue is visible at both ends and that the ends of the tube are inside the wood. To give a better surface for the adhesion between the brass and blank you can also roughen the brass surface with a light sanding before application of the glue. Then set the blank aside and allow the resin to set fully before proceeding.

Squaring up the ends

Before you can square off the blank its best to try to remove as much wood as possible using a band-saw (without touching the tube) after this there are I number if ways to square the blank, use a drill press fitted with a barrel trimming bit, or use a disc sander.

When I use this method (usually on harder woods) I like to start by roughly turning the wood to a cylinder. This way I get a centre mark for drilling, but am also able to role the blank on the sander platform which helps keep the end square.

Turning and Polishing the blank

Mount the blank on the lathe by inserting the bushings into the blank and the sliding the assembly onto the mandrel, for safety add several spare slim line bushings on at either end to give some separation from the large chuck / live centre and your hands.

fore the nut will help minimize potential bending of the blank along the mandrel which would result in a concentric pen rather than a round one.

Only tighten the nut on the mandrel once the end stock has been secured in place. For a single blank it's not so important especially if you shrink the mandrel down, but if you are turning a pen with two parts the securing the tail stock be-

When turning the blank start with a roughing gouge and keep the chisel turned away from me while turning the right hand side the rotate the chisel when turning the left.

The best advice you can get is to take your time, I've learnt from experience that working quickly will more often result I turned a simple barrel for the Purple Heart, but decided to add a small bead on the maple, to do this I switched to a small parting tool and made small cuts until I had a shape I liked.

in you splitting the blank, meaning a restart.

 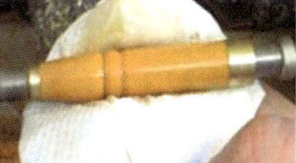

Polishing

Before polishing the blanks ensure that you have sanded them with increasing grades of sand paper, I like to combine the last grit (around 400 grit) with wax this not only completes the sanding but also starts to work the polish into the wood. It also works towards reducing the levels of fine dust as you finish your piece of work.

From this I move to a friction polish following the manufacturer's instructions and for the final coats I applied carnauba wax to give a hard shinny surface.

I find that carnauba tends to streak and clog if application and polish is done, so I try to keep the tissue on the turning piece at the opposite side to the wax stick and apply the wax as well as buff the piece at the same time. Working in this way reduces excessive application of wax and gives the right finish first time.

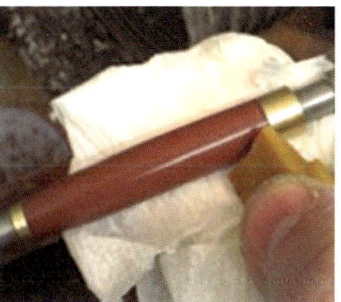

Alternate Finish

If you want a really shiny finish that's also very tough you could also use super glue (CA). To do this sand your pen as needed, (if you wish you can apply a sand and sealer, BUT no wax at this point). Place a drop of glue on a clean tissue and quickly work it over the surface of the barrel. Then apply a light sand and polish - for the polish I use either pen pads or friction polish. Note that sometimes you may need to very lightly sand with a fine grit paper to remove inconsistencies in the glue. Repeat this several times to get a tough coating. This can be a lot of work but gives great results.

A number of sources mention the use of medium thickness glue, but I seem to get the best results from household thin CA Glue. In addition to the glue you can also use a little Linseed Oil. put the oil on the tissue then put a single drop of glue onto the oil and apply to the pen. The oil helps to keep the glue from curing as quickly making it a little easier to work with, slight drawback is that it can take a little longer to finish the pen.

Assembling the pen

When you remove the turned pen barrel from the lathe it's a good idea to rub it ends on a piece of tissue to remove any build-up of wax that could interfere with the assembly. Also ensure that the epoxy resin, used to attach the blank to the brass tube, has not spread into the tube. If it has, remove it and clean up any edges with a fine grade sand paper. The consequences of not carrying out this check are that the turned material you have worked so hard on could split apart as you push the pen tip and other parts onto the barrel.

The tips of the pen tend to wobble during assembly so I drilled a hole in the middle of the plastic disk to hold the tip while it is pressed in place.

That's really all there is to it, once all parts are pressed together you can screw (in this case) or push the various pen sections together and enjoy your pen, or give it as a gift.

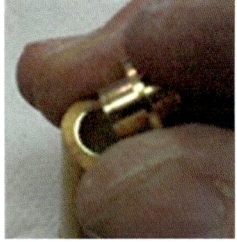 

To assemble the pen I have two bits of scrap plastic which I sit in a standard wood vice and slowly close the jaws with the two parts between. Using the plastic gives a better surface than the jaw face helping to keep the pen parts square to each other while they are being compressed.

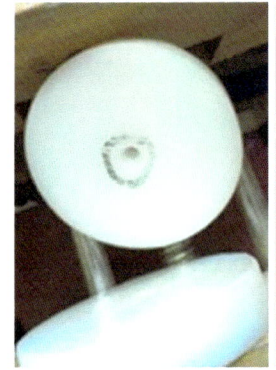 

 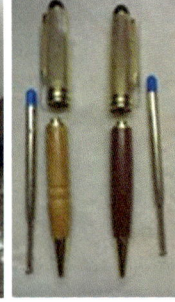 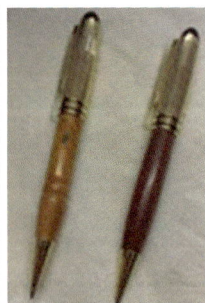

3: Wooden Christmas Bauble Tree Ornament

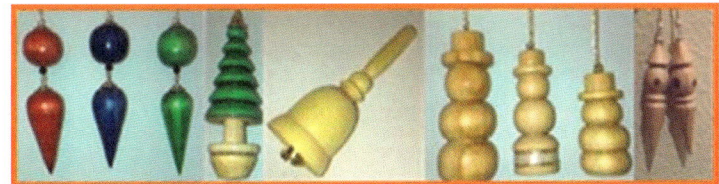

Christmas is a great time to practice wood turning as it seems that everyone wants something making, usually tree decorations. These are fun to make, producing something that can be enjoyed year after year. They also give you the chance to try out new techniques / ways of turning and you can make them as fiddly to make as you want.

What follows gives you an idea of the kind of decorations you can make – you can see more examples in the image above. Later on there will be another chapter on a more intricate decoration, a cube inside a bauble.

For this chapter I will be making a tear-drop decoration using two different woods.

Making the plugs

The first task is to cut a load of plugs from a wood that is different from that to be used in the main decoration (I used Mahogany). The cutters are nothing special they are generally available to make plugs used to cover screw heads in furniture such as tables and chairs. From the picture of the cutters – I used the round plug cutter (the four pronged type tend to damage the wood too much).

Pick an appropriate size of cutter and put it into your drill press then drill the wood till you are almost trough. Don't go all the way, that can lead to the plug flying out, and getting either lost or damaged.

Once you have drilled a sufficient number for your needs take a small grill bit or screwdriver and just flick the plugs free.

A Hobbyists Guide to Turning and DIY - Ideas for inspiration

Preparing the blanks

Next prepare your blanks, if you're making a few the get them ready together it saves time. Mark the centre's on each end, either by using a gauge, or by holding a pencil firmly and using your fingers as the gauge. Make several marks to ensure you have centre. This will help when it comes to turning to keep it stable in the lathe and also reduce wasted material while you do the initial rounding off.

Make a line on each piece of wood at a place where you want to put a plug, then mark the centre of that line and use a punch to define the crossing point. Use the punch at the ends as well to mark the centre point to line the wood up in the lathe.

Insert plugs

   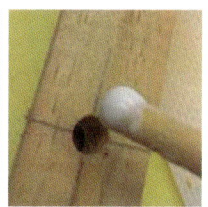

When ready measure the diameter of the plugs and drill holes at the crossing points on your blanks to match these diameters. Its ok to drill all the way through, at least for this project as the inserts will be on opposite sides of the finished decoration.

The place some glue inside the holes and ease the plugs into position. You will see that my easing tool was a hammer. If the plugs are a tight fit you should be fine to go on to round off the blank on the lathe, if not then you will need to wait while the glue sets before continuing.

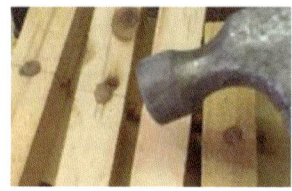

Turing your decoration

Once you have done all of the preparation it's time for the fun bit (wood turning) - Start by drawing a rough shape on a scrap of MDF and hold it level to the blank on the lathe.

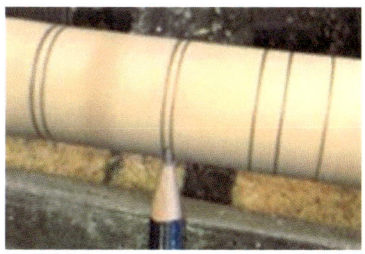

Then mark the blank at the points where the drawing change. A single mark gets a bit faint when turning so turn the lathe on and hold the pencil on the blank to make a line all the way around at each point then start turning using the drawing as a guide.

My first piece suffered a mishap - it split from the lathe (see pictures), but the others worked out fine. I applied a bit of polish before turning the point off. By applying polish before parting off the decoration is supported while you work.

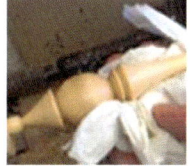 

Adding the hook

Part the decoration off of the lathe and used a small hand drill to make a hole in the top. The hook at the top is a piece of silver wire hand twisted using needle nose pliers and cut to fit the drilled hole. I like to add a bit of bling as well it hides the hole.

Even though the wire is held with glue a good tip is to put a kink in the wire that goes into the hole - it will hold more securely in the wood.

 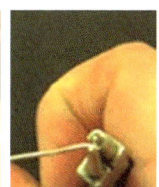 

Finishing the Bling

The decoration is finished off with a bead and a handmade spring.

To make the spring I used a 1.5 mm drill bit in a pin vice and wrapped a bit of the silver wire 7 times around it, then snipped the ends, and used long nose pliers to close up any gaps in the turns. A loop was formed on another bit of wire and the bead and spring slid on before a second loop was made at the top end. Open the lower loop slightly and close it again once the Top Bling is attached to the decoration. Apply some silver string to hang the decoration and its done ready for your tree.

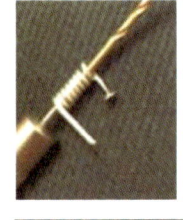

4: Wooden Cube in a sphere Christmas Bauble Tree Ornament

Making a cube inside a cube is a pretty simple activity; I thought instead I would make a Christmas ornament for our tree, the idea being to start off the cube and then turn the outside into a bauble, finishing by suspending the cube at the centre of the decoration.

Prepare the Wood

The wood MUST square to start with, if not then when you start to make the cube at the centre, it will be off centred which will reduce or remove the support it needs while you are working it on the lathe.

The material used was the leg from an old table, first I cut the end square on a band-saw then used the off-cut to set the size for the cube I needed by holding it at the end of the leg and pushing it so that the side of the off-cut was against the saw blade. I then used a sled on the band saw to keep the cut square and cut the cube. Once cut I made a mark on the centre of each face.

Start to form the cube at the centre

To cut the holes I used a kitchen door hole bit (short / wide Fostner bit) and a pillar drill. I made a hole at the centre mark on each of the faces. The depth was estimated at around the thickness of the main part of the cutter. When you do this try to keep each hole the same depth so that the cube in centred in the main block. Don't drill too deep or the corner joints will be too small to provide the extra support during turning. If you look at the picture you can see the corner joints on the centre cube and the holes at the side of the cube.

A Hobbyists Guide to Turning and DIY - Ideas for inspiration

Turning the Bauble

With all the holes drilled - I made a rough tennon on the lathe approximately the same size as the holes in the block. Don't remove too much wood as the block needs to be tight on the tennon during turning.

Push the cube onto the tennon all the way up to the centre cubes face then bring the tail stock up to the opposite side of the centre cube and start turning your bauble (only remove a very small amount at a time or you risk breaking the sides of the decoration and having to start over.

Once you have rounded the decoration remove the piece and start again by mounting another face on the tennon. Repeat for the three planes of the cube. With all of the turning done - carefully sand the bauble while it turns (watch out for your fingers).

Remove the bauble and use a sharp knife to gently remove the wood holding the cube at the centre, then sand the interior surfaces of the bauble and also the faces of the cube. Finally apply a finish - (I just used a sand and sealer)

Decorating the Decoration

When you drill the holes in the original block the bit leaves a dimple in each face of the centre cube, useful for lining up the tail stock during turning but not need to the seen in the finished piece. To hide this "production mark" I recycled some links from a charity shop bracelet and glued them over the holes, finally attaching a steel bead so that I could hang the bauble on the tree, this also allow me to suspend the centre cube in the middle of the decoration.

5: Wooden Christmas Carousel Ornament

Hand turned tree decorations are a great addition to your Christmas, but how about making a centre piece that also acts as a toy for your children. That is what this project is about. It will show you how to create a decoration combining a carousel with what would normally be tree baubles.

Because this was the first time I had attempted this and did not wish to waste material and time I decided to use the free Trimble Sketch up Program to design a 3 dimensional model to get an idea of how the carousel would go together. I have uploaded this to the sketch up 3d Warehouse if you wish to have a copy.

https://3dwarehouse.sketchup.com/model.html?id=ud4...

I then gathered the materials needed - all a recycled - either from other objects (tables, necklaces) or scraps left from other projects)

The carousel is made in three component types:

- Bases – Main Base and carousel base
- Pole – the centre of the carousel around which it will spin
- Ornaments – for this one two forms; snowmen and trees – but you could easily change this so that your decoration works for other celebrations.

Preparing the Bases

The base and the hanging platform where made from the top of an old table, mark out 2 squares (15x15 cm and one at 10x10 cm) then mark the centre of each with a cross and cut both out using a band-saw.

Drilling the centres

The platform would need to hang free from the centre post, so I used a short Forstner bit to drill part way into the centre of the 15 cm square. During turning the platform would be attached to the lathe chuck in expansion so I made sure that the bit was larger than the jaws I would be using. This would also ensure that the platform would hang free of the centre post once complete. I then drilled a 6mm hole at the centre

Attach the square to a scrap of MDF, and clamp this to the Band-saw with the blade against one if the sides. Turn the band saw on and slowly rotate the wood to remove the majority of the corners leaving a rough disk, take it slow as it's easy to rush and break your blade.

With the disc cut use the Forstner bit and drill all the way through the centre - the previously made partial hole allows for centring the bit on the disk. The disk was then finished on the lathe with it being held in place on the jaws with a scrap of wood against the outer face and the tail stock to keep it in place.

The Base

Once the disc for the base has been cut the hole required at its centre should be large enough for your lathes screw chuck, in this case 9.5mm. Once the disk is complete this hole will be increased to 10 mm for the central post.

Turning large discs

The first two images show the hanging platform. I removed most of the top material first (leaving the inner portion square, I then turned it over on the chuck. Because the inner section on the top the platform had been left flat the piece sat level on the chuck when turned. I then turned, sanded and finished the bottom of the platform before flipping it again to complete the shaping of the top and applying its finish.

The base of the stand was attached using a screw chuck, a spacer was added between the wood and the face of the chuck - this allowed me to remove more material before reaching the top of the screw chuck at the centre.

You can plan the shape as much as you like, but once you start turning its down to making what you like at the time so have fun with that part. For the finish I used a combination of sand and sealer, friction wax and Carnauba wax.

Parts for the platform and stand

The pictures show all of the parts for the platform and the stand.

The shaft was recycled from our children's old cot; it is approximately 20 cm in length to which was added a 10 mm tennon at the lower end to attach it to the base. I then re-drilled the hole in the base to 10 mm and once the shaft had been turned and finished it was attached to the base using the tennon and some glue. You will also need to drill a hole in the top of the shaft for the strings to support the platform.

Making Snowmen and Trees

The decorations on the platform would be Snowmen and Trees and to help get then the same size I turned two of each type at the same time.

First the Snowmen.

The wood must be held in the chuck and not between centres - important when you get to removing the decorations

Each Snowman would need 4 sections (Hat / Face / upper body / lower body)

Decide on the proportions and make a pencil mark on the wood for each section

Add a section to the bottom of the lower body for a tennon and also to allow for cutting the piece off.

Repeat the marks after the tennon for the second Snowman

Turn the lathe on and hold the pencil at each of the spinning marks to create a complete line around the wood.

Use the marks as guides - I like to use the tip of a parting tool to make a V shaped cut at each line to the depth I want the intersection to be and then shape each section (working from the centre of the section to the V cut)

I also added a cut in the top of the hat this was for some decoration on the hat at the end. Both Snowmen where then sanded and polished as much as possible; however the hats where still attached and so could not be completed at this point.

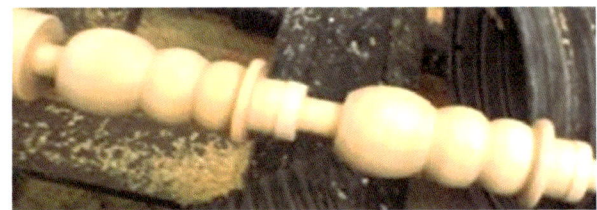

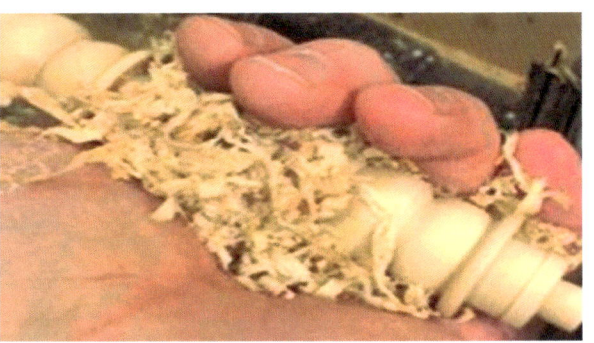

Removing the decorations from the Lathe

Start by removing the waste at the tail stock end – use a parting tool for this taking small cut until the area is clear. Support he decorations with your spare hand ensuring to keep clear of the chuck.

With the waste gone sand and finish the first snowman's hat and then part the first decoration from the lathe and move on to finish the remaining snowman in the same way.

The Tree's

The trees are made in the same way as the snowmen, but in re cherry for contrast. Once you have allowed for the tennon and the trunk of the tree start to cut a cone, don't cut all the way to the tip, this will be done later when removing the tree.

The levels of the tree are made by making V cuts as required. Again sand and finish both decorations as far as possible before starting to remove the individual trees (finishing the tops as you go)

Attaching the Trees and Snowmen

To attach the decorations measure the thickness of the platform and mark 4 equidistant points around its circumference - then drill four 10 mm holes at a depth of about 2 mm (important - not all the way through). With the holes made use the band saw to cut the tennons' to length and glue the decorations in place.

Adding some Bling

The platform is hung using strings from the top of the shaft to anchor points half way between each decoration on the platform.

Start by marking and drilling shallow holes to take the anchor wire and glue, for the holes I have a small hand drill. Now twist a loop on the end of some wire, or recycle a necklace and open one side of a link, cutting the wire to the correct length to fit the hole just drilled. Glue this in place. Repeat for all the remaining anchor points.

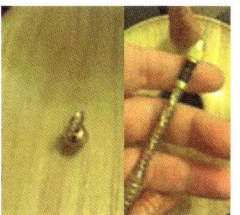

Now cut some gold thread (oversize it) and attach it to the bead decoration and when the glue on the anchors has set hook two of these in place - then pass the other end of the thread through the hole in the shaft.

To get the string to the correct length, support the platform at a height that is just free from the base, (this is the stationary height). Then adjust the length of the string so that it is equal on both sides of the central post. Ensure that when the length is measured you include the bead decoration. If you do not then the platform could rest on the base once finished and the platform will not spin.

The final addition is to add a bit of ribbon to the hat of each snowman for this use double sided tape on some ribbon and wrapped this around the hats putting a little glue at the ends to stop the ribbon from fraying.

With all strings the correct length, attach the anchor beads and glue these to the platform. Support the base while the anchor is setting, I find that Lego bricks work well for this.

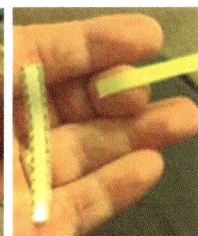

6: A Wand for Harry Potter - Magic

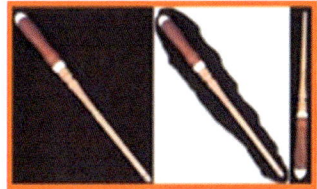

This project developed from a previous wand made as part of a birthday present for a friend of my daughter her being a fan of Harry Potter. That one was a two part design using beach for the wand and Mahogany for the handle, this wand will also include Velstone resin for decoration as well as a spiral pattern on the wand section. Note that wood turning does not have to be an expensive hobby all of the materials (apart from the glue) are recycled from other items – door frames, old cots etc.

The Wand "Stem"

The Magical part of the Wand is made from Beach reclaimed from my children's cot. The kids got bigger so we thought if a good idea to get larger beds - :-)

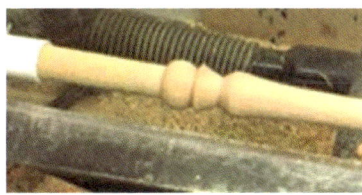

With the Tennon cut I completed a rough design for the remainder of the stem. Once I had a shape I liked I the piece from the lathe - but not before marking the wood close to the chuck with the number of the jaw that was touching at that point. – this would make it easier to remount the wood later for finishing.

Start by turning the tennon on a length of Beach, this would be used to mount the stem into the handle of the wand. As I would be using a 10mm Forstner bit for the tennon hole in the handle I measured that to get the exact diameter and then used the callipers to turn the tennon. Removing small amounts at a time until the jaws of the callipers moved over the wood.

Resin Decoration

The Wand would have two pieces of resin (Velstone offcuts from work tops) included in its handle. This material is also great for making pens when supported by a tube. The piece used was the waste from cutting an electric socket.

Prepare a blank (roughly square in cross section and long enough for the parts being made), then trimmed the ends to help when putting it into the lathe.

I then used the bench drill to make a small hole at the centre on one end.

This is very important (see Safety Note below)

One end of the Velstone went into the jaws on the lathe while the live centre on the tail stock was put into the indentation made in step 2.

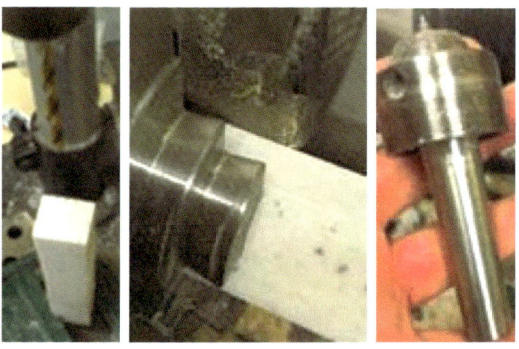

SAFETY NOTES

1. The velstone will be turned without substrate (i.e. no support as it would have when making something like a pen) - This means that it can be prone to fracture sending out flying particles.
2. Always use a face visor.
3. Because of the fracture potential the hole made at the centre on one end takes the point of the tail stock rather than winding it into the material as you would if using wood, however **DO NOT** over tighten as you can still split the material.

Turning the Resin Decoration

Start by rounding off the Velstone and apply some very basic shaping, then remove the tail stock and replace it the Forstner bit and turn the lathe back on. Advance the 10 mm bit slowly into the resin, withdrawing it at intervals to clear the waste. Once the hole is deep enough stop moving forward and leave the bit in place to support the material while you finish shaping the rings and polish them prior to parting them off. I made two to provide a spare in case of damage. To remove the rings use a hack saw instead of a parting tool to prevent the resin from shattering.

The second part needed from the resin was the capping at the end of the Wands handle. For this a tennon was made (10 mm) followed by an approximate shape at which point it to was removed from the stock material.

 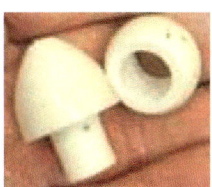

A Hobbyists Guide to Turning and DIY - Ideas for inspiration

Decorating the Stem

I did not know how long the tennon would need to be on the stem - so I used the marks made on the Stem before removing it from the lathe in step 1 to help centre it back on the lathe - I then extended the tennon previously made and parted it from the stock in the lathe jaws.

Next I attached one of the velstone rings to the tennon using Medium thickness super glue and once set I remounted the Stem in the lathe using the Tennon to hold it. The remainder of the shaping for the wand was then completed this included shaping and polishing the velstone to ensure a clean joint between the two materials.

I used a one of the micro turning tools from Robert Sorby to put a spiral along a portion of the wand followed by a bit of clean up using a sanding mesh. It was at this point that a mishap occurred:

While sanding I made the mistake of letting the pad get pulled from my hand - luckily I let go in time or the mishap would have been an accident. You can see the material spinning around the stem in the pictures. Once over that I put a little bulb at the end of the stem and darkened the joining line with a bit of Formica to form a friction burn.

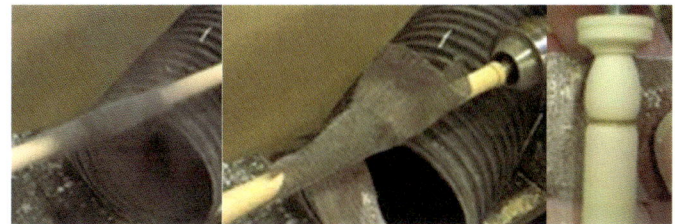

Finishing the resin handle end takes a bit of nerve as its mounted in the jaws with only a very small tennon to hold it, once you have a nice shape that's approximately the same diameter as the velstone ring, polished it using fine grade pen polishing pads. The important part here is to try to get the joining edge as square and sharp as possible to give a clean join when glued - The reason for this is that once attached it's the last bit and there would be no further opportunity to put it back on the lathe.

Getting a Handle on it

The handle is made from a small piece of reclaimed Mahogany left over from a previous project. I centre bored a 10 mm hole as before into one end as far in as possible, then cut a tennon on the same end. The wood was then turned around and held in the jaws while I repeated the drilling and shaping at the other end. An important note – the diameter of the handle ends must be slightly larger than that of the resin parts that will contact them once the wand is assembled – this gives room for a bit of error when finishing the handle. Use the Forstner bit throughout the shaping process to give support while working the material.

Trying to measure and get a flush joint when turning is difficult if not nearly impossible - In this case I did not need to - so to make the joint look good I formed a bead at the end rounding over the edge as the velstone was cut slightly smaller and rounded on the stem this would look good. I then sanded and polished this end as much as possible.

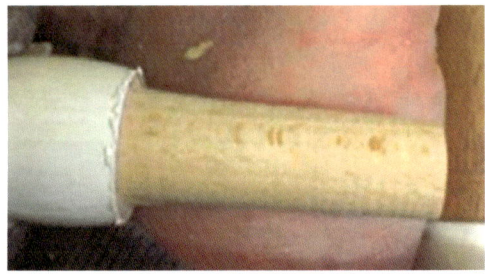

To turn the end that had been held by the chuck – I made a friction chuck from another piece of Beach and pushed the part made handle onto it (careful not to push too hard or the handle would split). I then brought the Forstner bit put and put it as far into the open hole as possible to support the wood again. All this allowed for turning and finishing the handle. Once complete the parts where assembled with the velstone capping held in place with super glue.

7: Spinning Top and Helicopter

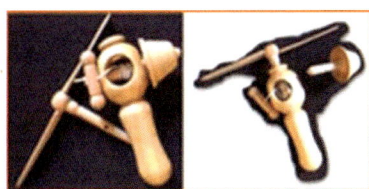

I've made a number of spinning tops in various shapes and sizes and have even made one with a handle and pull string. This chapter is intended to show how to make one of the pull string varieties. When I first made this form of top I used a slot for the string which meant that the end of the handle was wasted. For this one I want to use the end as a launcher for a toy helicopter. So this is to be two toys in one.

Spinning Top

Ordinarily to turn a spinning top I would make it from a single piece of stock. First forming the spinner and then turning the handle used to spin it and once sanded with a finish applied I would part it off and there you have it. BUT this top needs to be a bit stronger in the stem so I have made it in two parts.

Part 1 - The spinner

The first thing to do is centre drill a 10 mm hole that will eventually take the stem. I then turned a rough spinner shape; at this point it's not important to clean it up as it will need to be centred once the stem is attached. Once the basic shape is done form a short tennon where the point will eventually be and part it from the rest of the wood.

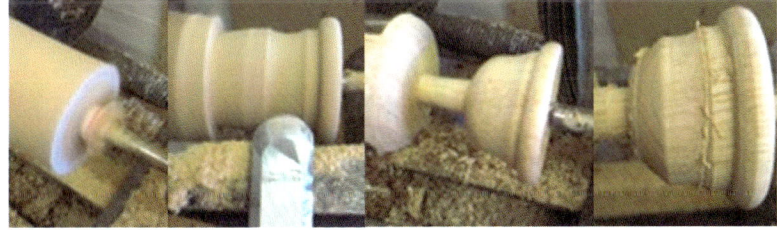

One of the tools used to shape the top was one I had made - just a plane chisel that I ground into a semi-circular end and sharpened to make a skew chisel that works in both directions without having to turn over.

Be careful when using a chisel like this (or any other) - if the tool bites in it will drag in one way or the other which can be quite a hazard. If you're lucky you only get to do some more turning, if not then you might need some medical attention.

A Hobbyists Guide to Turning and DIY - Ideas for inspiration

Part 2 - The Stem

Rough down a length of Beach, then form a tennon at the end. This needs to be 10 mm at the end; I gave it a slight tapper to help hold it in the spinner once the glue is applied.

With the spindle still in the lathe push the spinner onto the tennon and let the glue set. Bring the tail stock up to the end of the spinner and continue turning. First reduce the stem to less than 10 mm (it needs to spin freely the handle when the string is pulled. Then finish the rest of the shaping leaving the point until just before you part off the stem of the spinning top.

I've found that a slightly rounded tip is better for larger Tops; it helps them stay up for longer. A tip for polishing – if you use wood shavings to burnish the wood you get a smother finish, and the smother you can get this the better and longer it will spin.

Helicopter

A warning at this point:

The Helicopter MUST meet the following requirements for it to fly safely or at all

- The blades need to be as light as possible while keeping the post as heavy as possible, while still allowing it to spin in the handle, this helps to keep it stable.
- The blades need to be sufficiently large to provide the lift required for take off
- The blades MUST be a balanced as you can make them – if they are not then when you try to fly it the helicopter will turn around an give you a really bruised hand. I know I have had one.

If you don't think you can meet the above then don't give up on the spinner the hole in the handle works well either from the end or the side for the pull cord.

Kenneth Moore

1 - A Rough Shape

For the propeller I started by rounding off a dowel, and then formed a ball in the middle. Once I had the ball I used a ruler to mark off the length of the blade on one side and transferred that to the other then finished the turning to give a gentle tapper and removed it from the lathe

2 - Cutting the Blades

Next mark out a couple of lines off the centre separated approximately by 1 quarter turn, and draw diagonal lines from the edge to the tip of the blades. Using a band saw cut from the tip to the centre marks on both sides of the blades. Once you have both sides cut use the straight edge along the blade to gauge a parallel line then cut this piece away.

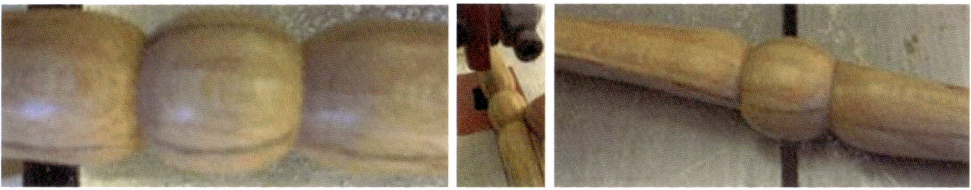

This will leave you with a rough blade that you can now sand and shape. Because I made cuts along diagonal lines the blades should be at a slight angle to each other - when sanding take care to keep this angle as it provides the lift for the helicopter.

3 - Attaching the Stem

Use the same 10 mm bit from the other holes and partially drill a hole in the central part of the blade and then attach the helicopter stem (I used thick super glue with and activator, but wood glue would work as well)

A Hobbyists Guide to Turning and DIY - Ideas for inspiration

Spinning Top Handle

1 - Holes in the Handle

You start the handle by drilling the hole for the stem of the helicopter to sit in, this is important as it sets the centre of the handle and helps you mark out the positions of the other two holes that need drilling. Once you have the correct depth (deep enough to take the whole stem) remove the piece from the lathe and move to the drill press. Next drill a hole large enough to allow you to thread the pull cord onto the stem. First take the helicopter - put it into its hole then hold the stem at the point where it meets the outer edge of the handle. Remove the stem and use the length from your fingers to the stem end to mark the depth of the hole in the handle.

Now mark the point for the large hole, it's important that the bottom of the stem is sat in a retaining hole or you will jam the helicopter when you pull the string so ensure to leave space from the edge of the bit you use. A 25 mm bit for this hole is sufficient, drill all the way through.

Rotate the handle to the adjacent side and make a 10 mm hole all the way through centred on the larger hole - this is the spinner hole. Test both holes by putting the relevant part in them and make sure that the parts spin freely.

2 - Turning the Handle

Remount the wood in the lathe and us a bit of scrap dowel inserted into the helicopter hole to give it more support while turning. Now turn a shape that's good for you. I general like a kind of skipping rope handle with a bulb on the end and for this one I made a little platform at the end for the helicopter. Be careful when turning the bulb as it's easy to catch the chisel on the rotating holes. When ready sand the piece and apply a friction wax finish to seal it then part it off of the lathe.

   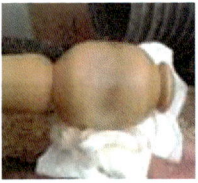

3 - Inside edges

Remember to take a bit a sand paper and remove splinters from inside the holes, also you will notice that the edges of the holes can be very sharp, remove this as well using the sand paper

Pull String

If you have a length of spindle with a 10 mm tennon on it (you should as you have just made a couple of stems and this will be scrap from those steps) then don't take the waste out of the lathe once you remove the handle, use it to hold this scrap - drill another 10 mm hole in the centre of the wood in the lathe and insert the scrap, bringing up the tail stock to hold the other end and help improve the friction fit. Then turn a small pull handle for the spinners.

   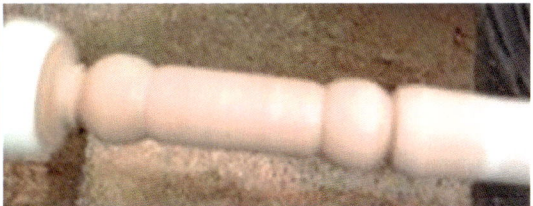

Threading the string

One of the last things to do is drill holes in all the parts that the string needs to go through:

- Spinner
- Helicopter
- String Puller

Start by putting the spinner into its hole in the handle and make a mark in the centre of the stem, then do the same for the stem of the helicopter. Now use the point of a drill to make a small hole - this will stop the bit from wondering while drilling.

Clamp the stem in a vice and drill the hole - the vice stops you mistaking your fingers for the stem. Drill the same size hole in all parts. The size will depend on the diameter of the stem and the string you will be using. Once the hole is in the Puller thread the string through and tie it around one half then push the not through the hole to hide it

Warning

Do NOT use the helicopter inside

Make sure to hold it over your head when you set it off, after all its a spinning piece of wood and with the string pull it gets to quite a speed.

Don't point it at anyone else

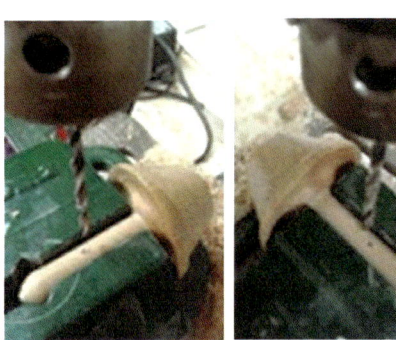

8: Hand Turned Tea light or Eggcup

We went to an outlet shopping village this weekend where I got some Yankee Tea Light candles and decided to make some bases / holders for them. The pictures above are the final outcome, I will leave it to you to decide if they are Tea-lights or Egg-cups, but I think they could serve both purposes.

Recycling wood and roughing down

The first thing to do is to mount you stock in the Lathe. For this project it was simple as the recycled table leg I used was both the right size to fit my jaws as well as being the size I wanted for the candle base.

I cut a length that would allow me to make more than one base and then roughed it down to a cylinder. Doing it this way helps to ensure that additional tea light bases made would be of similar size.

I also used a parting tool to square off the end near the live centre.

Marking up

The next task is fairly quick. Take one of the Tea lights and mark its depth on the outside of the wood. Then turn the lathe on and draw a line at the marked depth, then put additional lines at points along the length where you want the shape to change.

Turning the shape

Before you start to shape the outside you must make the hole for the candle. I used a Forstner bit in the tail stock chuck and drilled a hole deep enough to take the depth of the candle. The Bit I had was not quite wide enough so I had to finish the hole with a scrapper.

With the hole cut I removed the chuck and put the live centre back on the tail stock and used the spike hole made by my drill bit to centre the tail stock. This is a good idea as it supports the wood while you turn and finish the outside shape.

Now use the lines that you made earlier to put a shape on the piece that you like

Burnishing

Once you have finished shaping the piece, get some of the shavings from the floor (by now you should have quite a few) and carefully press them onto the spinning piece. This has the effect of removing most if not all of the scratches in the wood and you are left with a very smooth finish.

Adding a pattern

The basic piece was a little plain so a pattern was needed for this a small curve in the stem, then a rotating cutter was used to form a spiral pattern. Once happy with the design, I used a parting tool to square off on either side of the spiral. Finally a stiff bristle brush was used to remove any imperfections in the spiral.

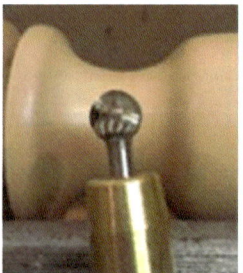 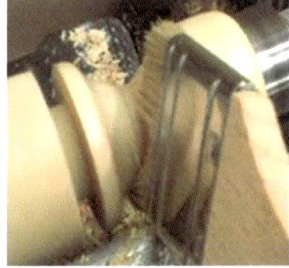

With that done I applied some friction polish and buffed the base finishing this step off by once again burnishing with the wood shavings and parting the cup from the stock was done.

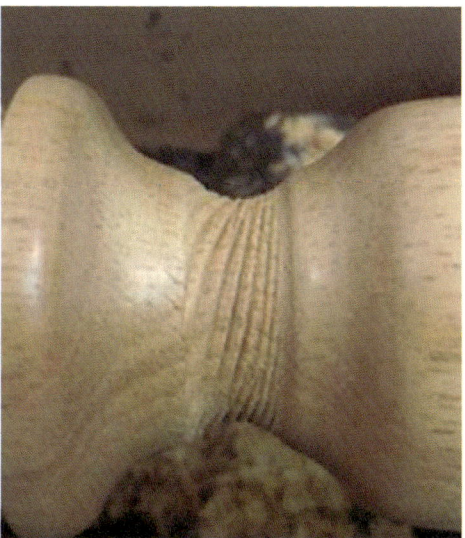

Note - If you cut slightly at an angle during parting off your finished piece will stand level of flat surfaces, it should also require less effort to remove the small nib of wood left when it finally comes off.

Once you have put all the effort in what is left is something that attractive and useful and could either be and egg cup or a tea light. That choice is up to you.

A Hobbyists Guide to Turning and DIY - Ideas for inspiration

9: Recycling paper to make seed pots

Paper seed pots are a great way to recycle your newspaper or any other biodegradable rubbish that comes through your letter boxes these days to save you money and effort when planting seedlings. The options for DIY include origami and hand rolling cylinders and folding over the edge. However if you want a consistent, easy method then you need some form of jig to do the job. Please note that this is not unique you can buy commercial versions of this project, this is just my interpretation.

Recycling

The material used in this project was reclaimed from an old coffee table, the rest of the table being used for other turning activities, for example the Tea Light in the last chapter.

To make the best use ensure that you accurately find the centre - I used a simple template available from most DIY shops, but if you don't have one then use a straight edge across the corners. If your material is off-centre then mark as many centre lines as you need to get a good approximation of the centre point.

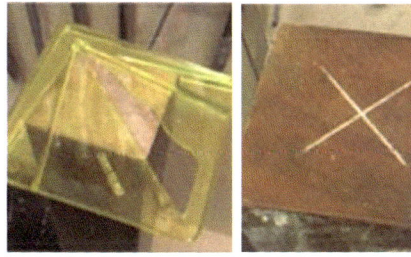

Once you have the middle at both ends use a punch to make a guide point for the lathe centres and mount the wood on the lathe.

Use a roughing gouge to start and then moved onto a skew chisel, you can see that my leg has a notch cut where it was held to the table take care on areas like this the chisel can easily bite in, giving you a bit of a kick.

Check you have fully rounded your stock by resting the back of the chisel on the rotating stock - if it bounces then you still have some work to do.

Prep the blank

Once the stock is round (or nearly) cut a tennon at one end. Make sure to include a slight taper this will allow the jaws of the chuck to grip the wood securely. Then remove the stock from the lathe and remount using the jaws to hold the tennon. Mark out the areas on the wood where the turning will change direction and use a parting tool to start cutting the wood down to a manageable size, I tend to remove it from the lathe when I get to a point where my band- saw can finish off.

Jig - Pot Former

Start by reducing the diameter of the stock by approximately 1 cm – this is to allow the former to fit inside the base. This need to be done as the whole piece is being made from the same starting material, then mark off the height of the former it's up to you, but I think that about 5 to 6 cm should be fine. Then turn a bulb on the end to give the piece a handle - it also helps with the overall look.

Once you have the former turned to the required diameter make an indentation into the base leaving a rim of about 0.5 cm around the outer edge. This will allow the paper to deform when pressed together to help give support to the finished seed pot. Before parting the piece from the stock burnish with wood shavings and a little friction polish - this will give your jig a longer life.

Base of the Jig

Use the remaining stock already mounted on the lathe and mark off two circles on the face of the base.

- The radius of the outside of the Former, and
- The radius of the indentation on the Former

Then remove the material between the two lines to give me a "trench" for the former to sit. Make the depth of the trench approximately 1 cm it should not need to be more that this for the jig to work

The raised circle of wood in the middle will help press the paper into a rigid shape when making the pots. It need to be reduced until it was about 2 to 3 mm higher than the base of the trench and will fit inside the indentation on the Former when it is in use. You are free to add any decorative curve to the outside of the base prior to finishing

This is going to be a working jig so fine sanding and polishing are optional, however the better the finish the longer left this piece will have and so the more pots you can make with it. At the very least you should burnish the surface to remove the risk of splinters during use.

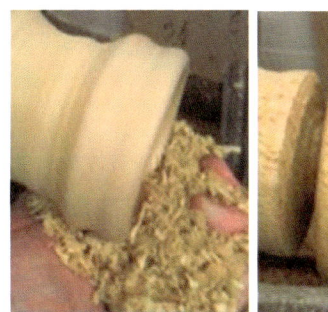

Finally part off the base from the lathe and finish the centre off with a little sanding..

Using the Seed Pot Jig

The jig is a tool that will last you years and hopefully save a lot of pennies while helping to recycle the rubbish. To use it you need to cut (or tare) a piece of paper long enough to wrap around the Former approximately 1.5 to times, it also needs to be wide enough to overhang the bottom of the Former.

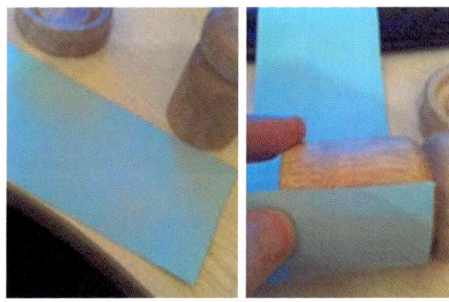

Wrap the paper around the former and push the overhang around the bottom, then holding the paper in place push the Former into the base and start to rotate, applying pressure at the same time.

Once happy with the pot carefully remove it from the Former. To help hold the top of the pot together bend over the top rim this also helps give the pot a bit more strength.

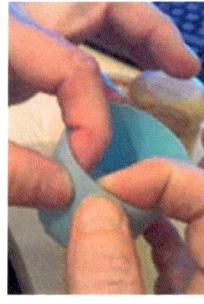 

All that's left is get planting your seeds - and once they start to grow you simply plant the whole pot into the soil and let it disappear as the plant grows out of it.

10: DIY Drum Sander

This is a short guide to help with something I don't like doing: Sanding. It's not the most interesting part of any project, unfortunately it's the part that can either make or break the look of the finished job.

On several occasions I have found a need to sand around corners or to sand an edge so that the resultant surface was square. That's why I came up with a couple of ways to do most of my sanding quickly and to a high standard using variations on a single drum sander design that can be adapted for either lathe or drill press usage.

The Drum

For the drum you have a three possible options

Dowel – good for sanding awkward parts.

You can get some fairly large size diameter dowel - the benefit is that it's already round, the drawback is that you have to find a way to centre drill it so that you can mount on you tools. My suggestion would be to use this as a hand sanding tool - cut a length long enough to give you a handle as well as space for attaching the sand paper

Bench Drill

If you don't have a lathe this is a relatively quick way to make the sanding drum. Use a large hole cutting wood bit and drill into a piece of wood for deep sanding drums double up on the wood this will give you the round drum complete with a centre hole. Attach a bolt through the centre with a large washer on each side. Next mount it in you bench drill and sand the drum while it is spinning.

Lathe

If you have a lathe you don't need to do either of the above. Mount a bit of stock between centres and turn it to a drum (sanding as required. If you want to mount it on a drill you can either use the marks left by the lathe centres make a hole, or turn a spigot on one end and remount the piece on the lathe using jaws then centre drill the wood while it's spinning on the lathe.

Note: for drum sanders to be used on bench drill you need to consider the capability of the drill - the sander cannot be as large as it would be if used on the lathe

Once you have the drum glue sandpaper to it. With the pieces still on the lathe this makes an excellent drum sander for small pieces of work where fine control is required.

You are not limited to one grade of paper, it's a good idea to make the drum large enough to apply multiple grades – this means that you will not have to change drums as you need move through the sanding grades.

One word of warning for both sanders get the cantering correct or the vibration can be annoying or possible damage your projects.

Attach the sand paper

Once you have the drum for use on either drill, lathe or by hand, attaching the sand paper gives a couple more possibilities.

Glue – You could just make a number of drums and attach different grades of paper to each using glue - this is good for one off use, but does mean that you have to swap drums to change paper. Or

Velcro – If you have sand paper that has the Velcro backing then glue the hook part of the Velcro to the drum this gives you a sander that does not need to be removed from tool to change the sanding grade - simply replace the paper for finer grit or as it wears out

11: Up from the Ashes a Mantel Piece renovation

This project started life as an accident. The original intent was to strip back the paint from an existing mantel piece. Unfortunately the previous owners had painted and re-painted the whole fire place and finally drilled into it to block it off, all of which made cleaning difficult. After trying and having little luck I decided to remove it to see if it could be taken to a specialist for stripping. That's when everything fell to pieces (literally). What I thought to be marble was in fact slate that was so old that crumbled as I attempted to lift it from the wall.

A real shame, but at least this made it easier to clear away and also allowed for the removal original Iron. **For Safety (in case there was any lead present)** I moved this to the garden so that it could be cleaned. Starting with a jet wash to remove most of the paint and finished it with a wire brush and drill combination - at all times wearing a dust mask to avoid possible lead in any of the blacking or subsequent paint layers.

The iron was framed with its original tiles, these too had years of paint on them. The tiles where removed prior to jet washing the iron and worked on separately. "**Top Tip**" I found that the best thing for cleaning the paint from the tiles is to use oven cleaner, when left lifted the layers without much effort. Once all sections had been cleaned I reassembled the iron and primed it.

Starting at the top

As the proportions for the whole mantle would come from the top, this was the starting point for construction. The original mantle overhung out into the alcove on one side of the fire place. This looked too large and also made decorating difficult, so the top would be reduced slightly. As this was to be a decorative piece, not functional MDF would be used for most of the construction, with a little wood thrown in for decoration

For the top I cut three boards (2x 18 mm and one 9 mm - Picture's 5 and 6. Using a router and round over bit to shape the sides and one of the long edges on both of the 18 mm boards.

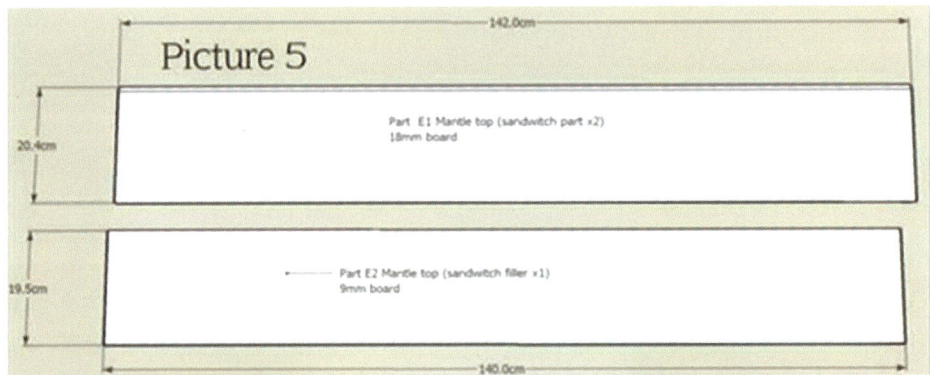

The 9 mm board was cut square and made smaller than the 18 mm sheets. (Picture's 7 and 8) The boards where sandwiched together using clamps all the way around to ensure even contact between the surfaces (Picture's 9 and 10).

Side Columns

With the top made I was able to set the sizes for the rest of the sections (Pillars, front plate and base). This allowed me to list all of the sections and get my D.I.Y. store to cut the larger parts to help speed construction.

Next to be made where the pillars, these where formed from four parts, a front, 2 sides and a base plate. I made the outer sides slightly wider than the inner, this was to enable me to bed the finished mantle against the wall and plaster up to the side without leaving a gap. (Pictures 11, 12, 13 and 14).

To help support the sides I used some off-cuts spacing them up the front of the pillar, putting the last one at the top of the inner side, this would help to support the front plate once attached. The front plate was a single piece of 18 mm MDF, this is important as it forms the main support of the mantle giving it all of its strength. It was also used to set the width of the mantle as it fits across the whole of the pillar. (Picture 12)

Once the front plate was in place I set the last piece of the inner frame across the top between the pillars. This was done in this order to prevent the edge of the MDF from being visible.

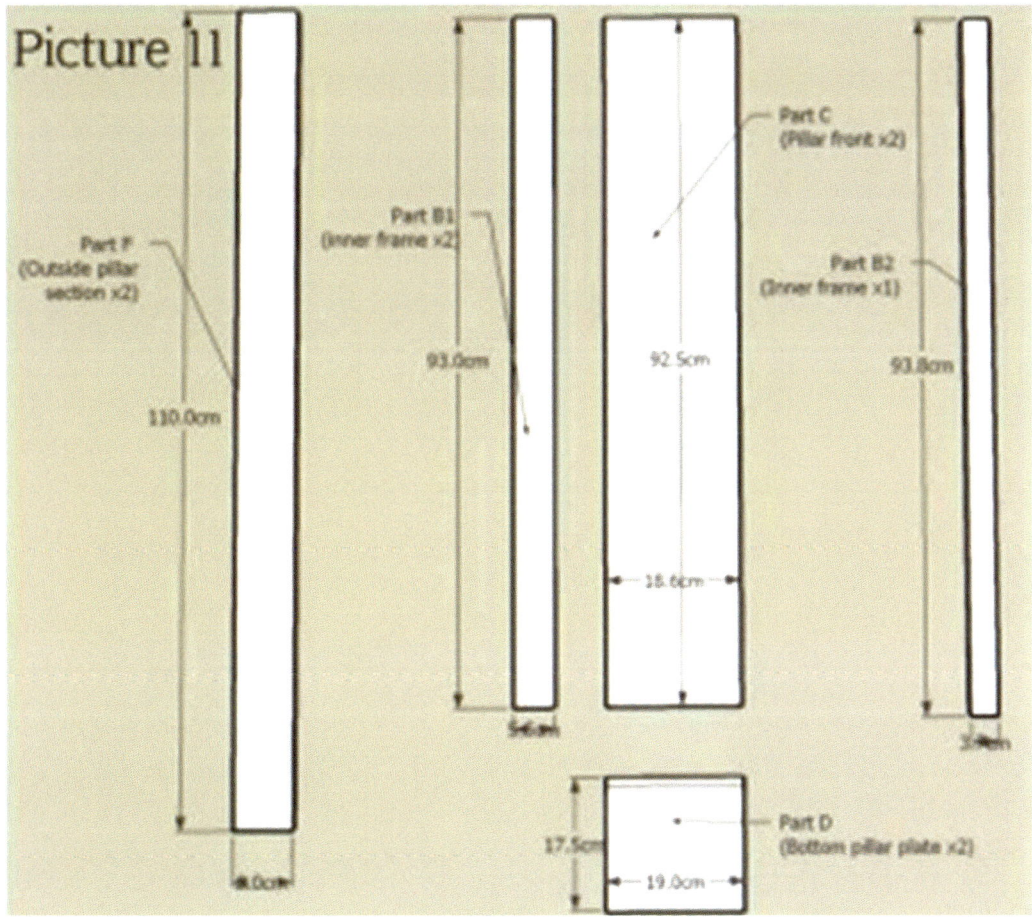

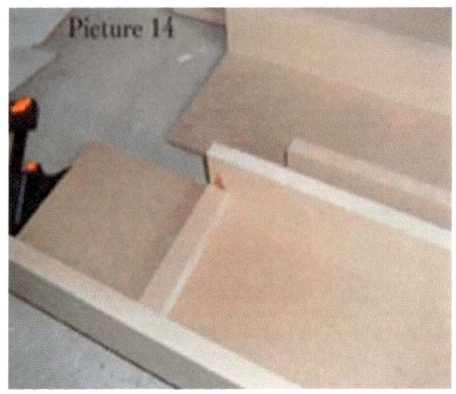

Make sure that the parts are square during construction or this will cause difficulty when putting it all together. For added strength and to help in aligning the parts I added some pre-cut bits of wood on the inside of the columns

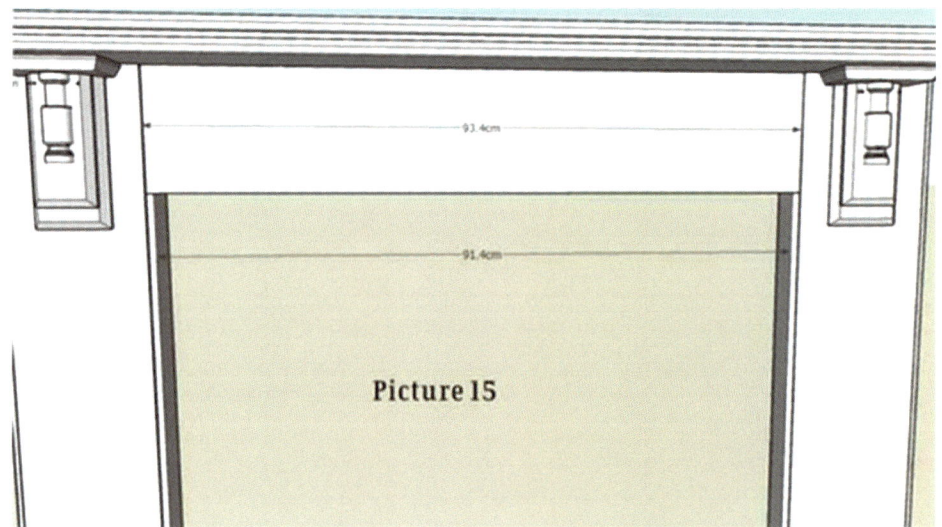

The Base

The Base was next for construction and, due to the layout and number of measurements required probably the most complicated part. To start I placed the Iron back into the hole in the chimney. Then put a straight edge across the front and made multiple measurements from the straight edge to the back of the iron.

Each measurement was marked onto the straight edge along with the distance between measurements. I started from the middle and worked out; this meant that I only had to measure one side assuming that the shape would be symmetrical. I then used Google Sketch-Up to draw the vase out to see if it looks correct (Picture's 16 and 17)

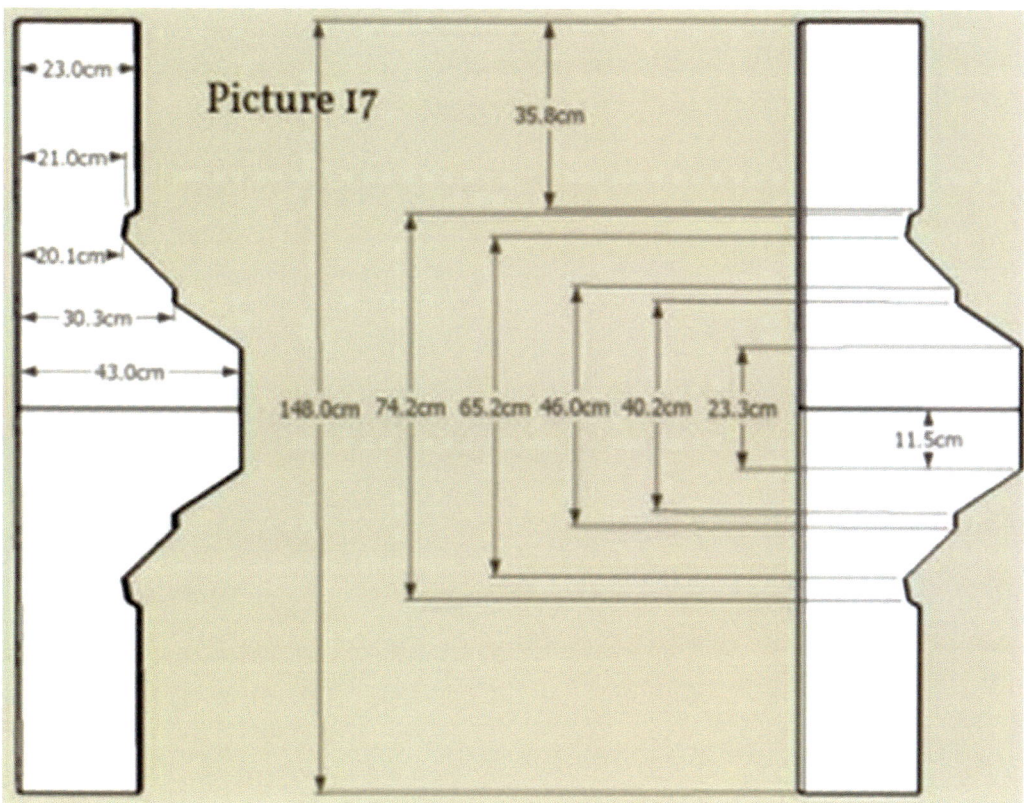

These measurements where then transferred to a sheet of 18mm MDF and the base cut out using a fine tooth jigsaw blade. (Picture 18) and a router was used to both round over the bottom of the base and put a curve into the top edge.

With this complete I cut some rough strips of MDF and attached these to the underside of the base as a frame. This would form the platform to lift the base off of the floor to make it easier to fit carpet later. (Picture's 19, 20 and 21)

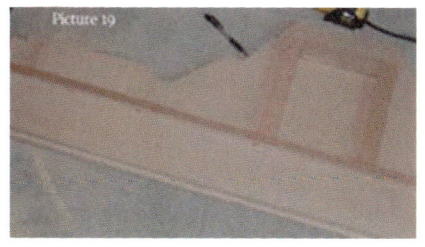

A Hobbyists Guide to Turning and DIY - Ideas for inspiration

Building the Mantle

This was the easy part using a combination of glue and screws I fastened first the base to the floor and then the pillars and face plate to the wall using stop blocks inside the base of each pillar to ensure correct positioning. I used the original wall ties to secure the top of the pillars.

The top of the mantle was fastened using screws placed as close to the brickwork as possible to hide them once the wall was plastered.

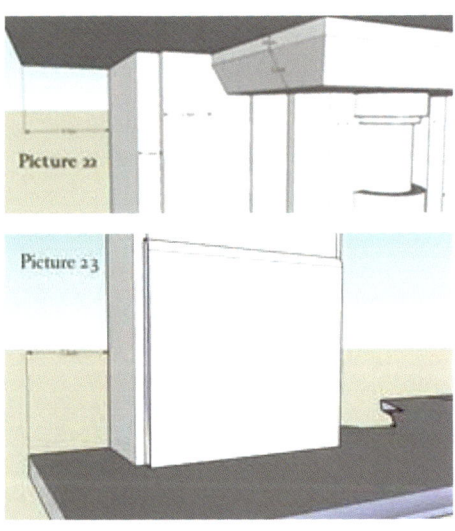

Decoration to the rescue

While building the mantle in the previous step noticed that I had made an error in the depth of the pillars they were not large enough to support the mantle top, which could have meant starting from scratch, however decoration came to the rescue. I decided to add some corbels; these would provide the support I needed as well as give the mantle a decorative feature.

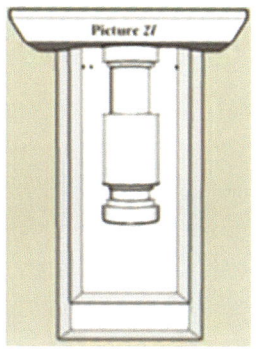

For the decorative "screw cover" I had previously obtained some banister spells while at the local tip these were split in two on the table saw in the safest way possible.

First I made a jig to hold the spells and then used the table saw with the riving knife removed to allow the jig and spell to be cut using the fence of the saw as a guide. Working this way prevented the spell from wondering as the blade moved past the it's square edges. The jig was made overly long to provide a handle to hold it safely away from the blade and a stop block to remove the need to hold the spell in place during cutting (all other precautions were taken – mask, face visor etc.)

Each corbel was made from four parts. Three of which would provide the strength and the final part would hide the screws attaching them to the mantle as well as adding to the overall effect. (Picture's 27,28 and 32) cut the three pieces of MDF to size using a table saw to put an angle on three of the edges on each of the parts.

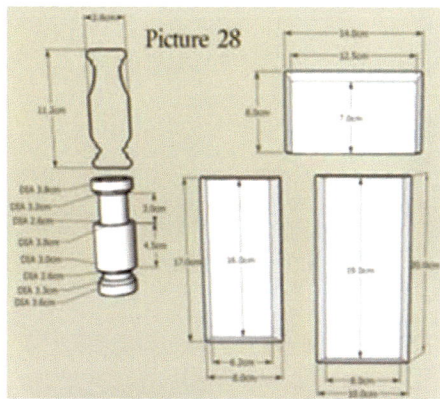

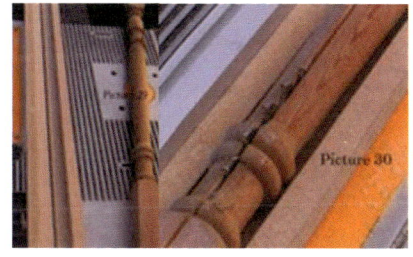

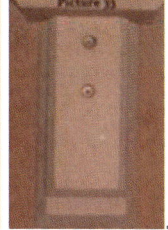

A Hobbyists Guide to Turning and DIY - Ideas for inspiration

The decorative part needed for the corbel was cut to size using a chop saw, with all of the parts cut (Picture 32) the corbels were glued and screwed together. The corbels where attached to the columns in the same way (Picture 33). The final unit would look as per Picture 34.

Blocking in the Fire Place

The next task was to block off the fire place.

However before this I wanted to know what, if anything was left up the chimney. Instead of pocking my head up there I cheated and held my digital camera through the hole with full flash.

I wanted this to be a light weight fitting to enable removal at a later date should I need to clear any fallen debris from the rear of the fireplace, so once the picture had been examined I blocked the fire place hole using 9 mm MDF using a scrap of wall paper to draw the contour from the fire iron, and transferred that to the material ready to be cut on a band-saw.

I used a router to put a decorative curve to the parts and mitred them so that they fit correctly into the recess left by the original fire blocks. The parts where held in place using no-nails which could also be smoothed out removing the need to sand before painting.

The Finished Mantle Piece

The only tasks left where to trim the inner edge around the iron with some wooden Dado Rail, Plaster the surrounding wall and apply a finish.

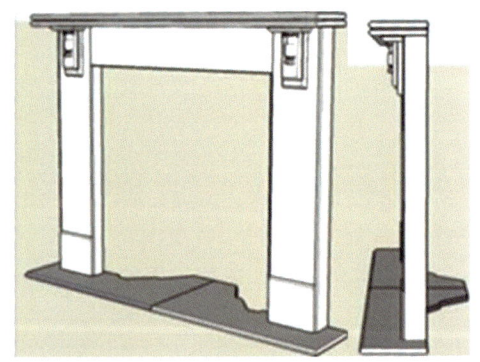

12: Door Trimming Jig

One problem with having an old house is that doors and their frames all tend to be handmade to fit whatever hole had been left by the builder. As a result the word standard size means little.

Now it's not too difficult to add wood to a door to increase its size, but removing can get tedious, especially having to use jig or hand saws. A jig is probably the easiest way to get around this and give you a repeatable result. The following very simple jig for an electric hand plane is one such idea.

Jig Parts

The jig is made up from two separate parts

The Plane "frame"

Take your electric hand planer and on a piece of paper trace the shape of the motor case, then transfer this shape onto a piece of 12mm MDF. For ease ensure that the edge of the shape closest to the cutter is placed along a straight edge of the MDF. It will be this edge that runs along the rail / runner of this jig.

Cut out the hole to leave a space to fit the motor case of the planer, Its getter to have a snug fit than a loose one, keep this in mind when making the hole. You planer should also have a hole in it to attach an edge guide, use this as a guide to drill through the MDF and secure the planer to the material with a suitable nut and bolt.

The Rail / Runner

The rail is made from two more pieces of MDF, the length of which must match that of the largest door you will be trimming.

12 mm MDF Parts	
Part 1 :-Rail guide	1 cm wide
Part 2: -Frame cover	3 cm wide

Glue and screw the two pieces together to form an "L" shaped rail or runner. Once the glue was set drill a series of holes through both lengths – to be used to secure the rail to the door using small screws

Set up and Use

Ensure that the frame is securely attached to the planer also that the cutting surface is parallel to the MDF straight edge. Measure the distance from the heel of the planer parallel edge of the frame, a set gauge will help ensure accuracy for this. Use that distance to fasten the rail to the face of the door checking the distance with the gauge before putting each screw in. Insert the edge of the frame into the runner, with zero cut set it should just move nicely along the rail. If it snags at any point just loosen the closest rail securing screw a little. Adjust the cutter depth as you would normally (depends on your particular tool) to the amount to be removed and start plaining until the frame edge meets the rail. If more material is to be removed that the depth of the gauge and the max set point for the planer, simply attach the rail to the door as required to complete the cut. This jig will also work well on tappers for e.g. chair or table legs.

13: A Motor Bike - What a Rocking Ride

This toy was made for our son to have fun on although it was used by all of our children. From the pictures, it's a stylised motorbike complete with motor sound effects provided by the rider. I found the original while on holiday and rather than buy it (too small) I decided to make one and adjust its design to suit. The first thing to do was to take a couple of pictures of the original to help with proportions. I split the bike into it component parts and drew up a set of templates in scale with the pictures previously taken, then set about making it.

Templates and initial model

I started with squared paper setting a scale from the photos – this didn't work so I decided to take the main measurements and draw the templates freehand, these where refined until I was happy with the curves of the bike. I then photocopied the originals and made a miniature model to ensure that the parts would work when assembled, rom the model I decided that the front wheel arch was too square so I adjusted it on the original templates. What I could not tell was the size of the slots in the rocker supports – this would depend upon the thickness of the final material used in the full scale toy.

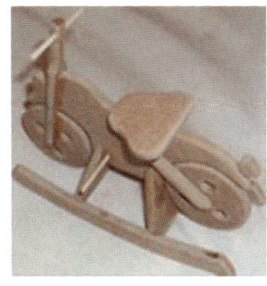

Once satisfied that the templates they were enlarged using a photocopier, up to four times the original size (depends on the child's size). Example use the inside leg measurement of the child then added a little to allow for increase as they get older.

Transfer the finished templates to a piece of hardboard, then cut out the shapes on a band saw for the rough cut and a jigsaw with a fine blade for the detail.

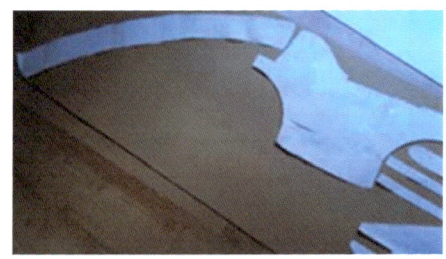

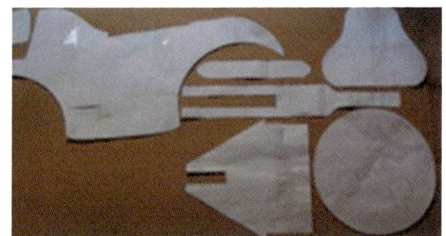

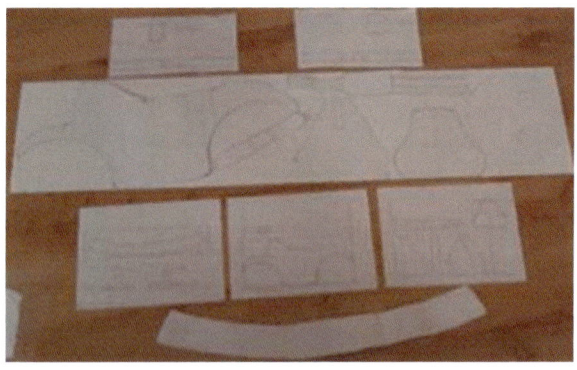

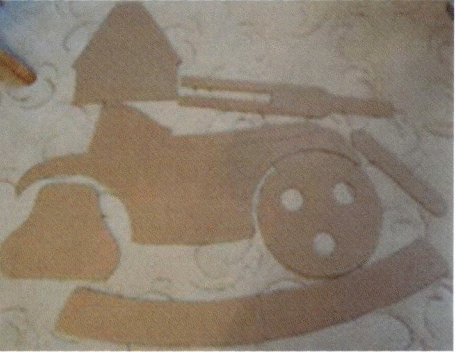

Kenneth Moore

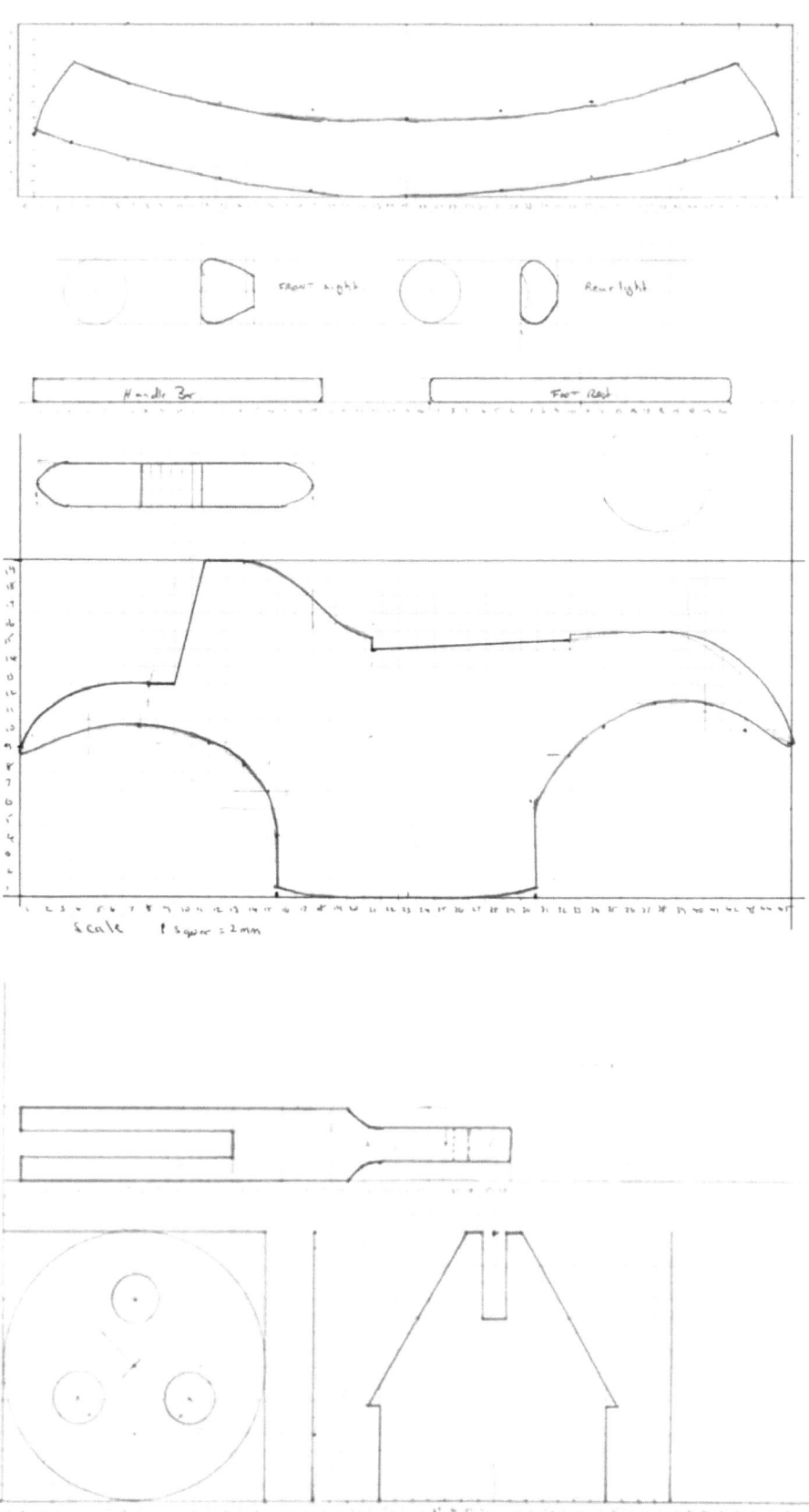

Laying out the parts

With templates cut lay them out on the timber and draw around them, trying to get the pieces as close as possible to avoid waste. Then cut each part using a Jig saw. If you mark the centre of the wheel template with a small drill hole, this will help to centre the finished wheel.

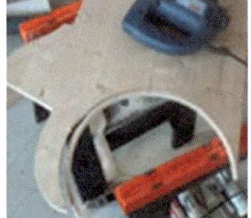

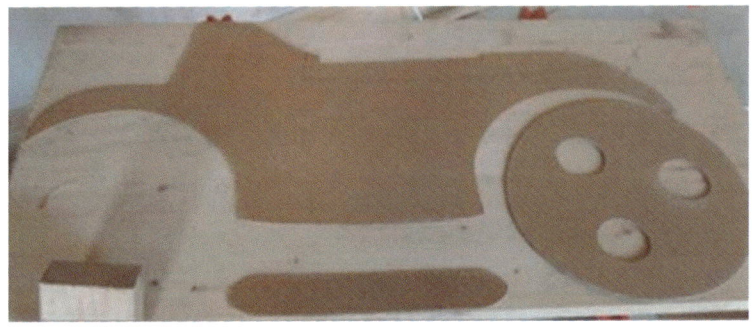

With the wheels cut it was time to start on the forks and rear struts. I chose the easier rout and went for the struts first. These where cut from the same board as the wheels using the templates. I then used my cross-cut saw to form a recess in one side of each strut. This would let the wheel to spin once assembled.

clamps then holes were drilled all the way through and dowels inserted to make sure that the struts could not move. A further hole was drilled through the ends of the struts and the wheel centre and the wheel attached using a dowel and glue, clamps were used to push the dowel in place.

After sanding all of the parts for the rear wheel assembly the struts were glued in place, holding them using quick grip

The Seat

The seat was made in the same way as the other parts using the templates, once cut the edges where rounded over using a router an to secure the seat to the body to the bike a combination of dowels and glue blocks was employed.

Mark a centre line on the underside of the seat and drilled three holes to take the dowels. Then use dowel points in the holes to mark the positions for the holes on the body of the bike. Then it was a simple matter to glue and clamp together. While the glue is setting cut some glue blocks to provide extra support and attach then between the body and the underside of the seat. If required use a couple of pins from a nail gun to hold the blocks while they set.

Front Forks

There are a couple of ways to make the forks for the bike; Join three separate pieces together and shape as required, or use a single piece and some method of cutting it to shape.

This time a table saw was used to cut a single block. The space between the forks was set to just larger that the thickness for either the wheel or the body of the bike. With all of the cutting complete (forks, post shoulder etc.) drill a hole for a large dowel handlebar (length of broom handle) and then sand / finish the part. The hole will be a tight fit so a little persuasion may be needed. If your hole is a little large then secure the bar in place with the help of a dowel (see picture) More dowels are used to attach the forks to the main body of the bike using the same method used on the seat. Once set turn the bike upside down and attach the front wheel and the rocker supports.

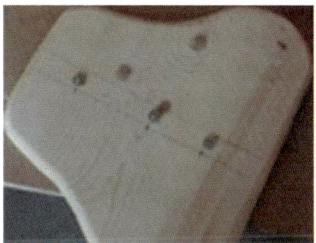

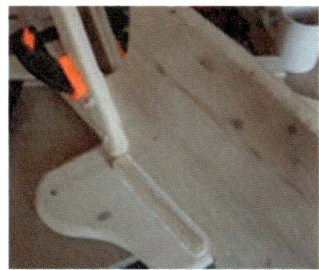

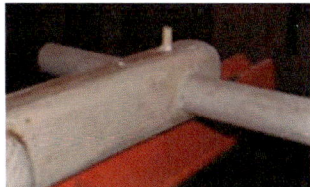

Rockers

Had I have thought about it I would have used my router with a long bit and a template guide to cut the rockers, but instead I did it the hard way using a jigsaw to cut each of the two rockers, I then clamped them together and used a belt sander to ensure that they were both the same size and shape. As the rockers would be under quite a bit of stress in use these are the only parts that were held in place using glue and screws

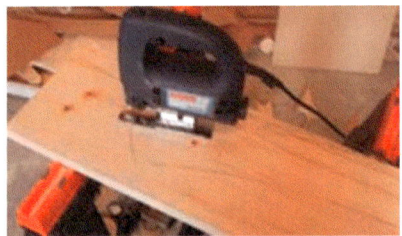

Lights, Motor and Finish

With all of the main parts made it was time to make accessories, these were carved using an electric chisel.

Lamp

First draw circle onto a piece of MDF the same size as the front of the lamp, the wood is then clamped over this and the chisel used to remove the material until the circle below can just be seen. The rest of the lamp is carved by eye. Note that before starting to carve first cut the correct angle for the lamp to attach to the bike using a crosscut saw – this would be dangerous to attempt once the parts have been shaped. The lamps where sanded and held in place with dowels.

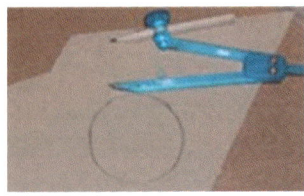 

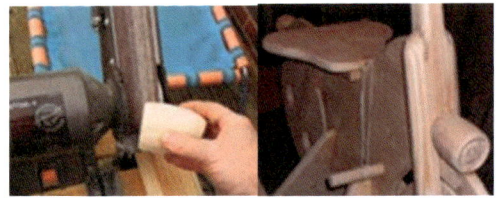

Motor

The motor was an afterthought as the original design was missing a part that made it look like a motorbike. Cut a piece of paper to fit onto the part of the bikes body where the motor would go. Then draw a rough shape for the part. Using the same wood and a jigsaw cut two motors (one for each side), then carve them in the same way as the lamps and as with the other joints on the bike glue and dowel them in place.

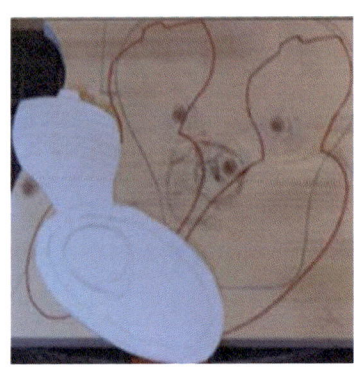

Foot Rest

The last part to put on was the foot rest this was a piece of broom handle larger than the handle bars and glued through a hole drilled in the body of the bike. It is held in place until the glue sets with a piece of string to keep it level with the body.

Finish

The finish for the bike was a combination of stain, yacht varnish and child safe paints and resulted in a toy that looks old fashioned but is bright enough to grab the attention of a two year old.

A Hobbyists Guide to Turning and DIY - Ideas for inspiration

14: Hobby Horse

This toy started life as a statement from my first daughter. One day she saw a horse on television and stated that her daddy could make her one of those. Being a little under 2 years old (at the time) I thought that this was a bit of a whim and that she would forget. However after a few more requests and a couple of orders I decided that it might be a toy she would play with and get some enjoyment out of. No sooner had I finished it than she tried to feed it after having sat it, upside down, in her toy high chair, she continued to have fun with it for quite a few years after that.

When we had a second daughter and I decided to make another so both could play together.

This was the first toy I had attempted and I didn't really know how to go about it, so I started by sketching what I thought would be a simple horse head shape, with the finished article intended to be a rocking horse, but latter changed this to a Hobby Horse as it would be more mobile and hold more interest because of it.

Templates

From the initial sketches the head consist of five sections, which were transferred to a grid with a scale of 1 square = 4.96 mm, diagonal length = 7.01 mm. From this the templates for the sections were created by tracing the parts onto some scrap hard board which were then cut out on a band saw.

The first horse was made from some scrap pine, which has lasted well, but does show a few dents and pits. So the horse next one was made using a hard wood. A local wood shop was selling some recycled shelves which were great for the job only requiring the varnish to be removed off with an orbital sander

Recycling:

A Hobbyists Guide to Turning and DIY - Ideas for inspiration

These are the final templates created for the horse head.

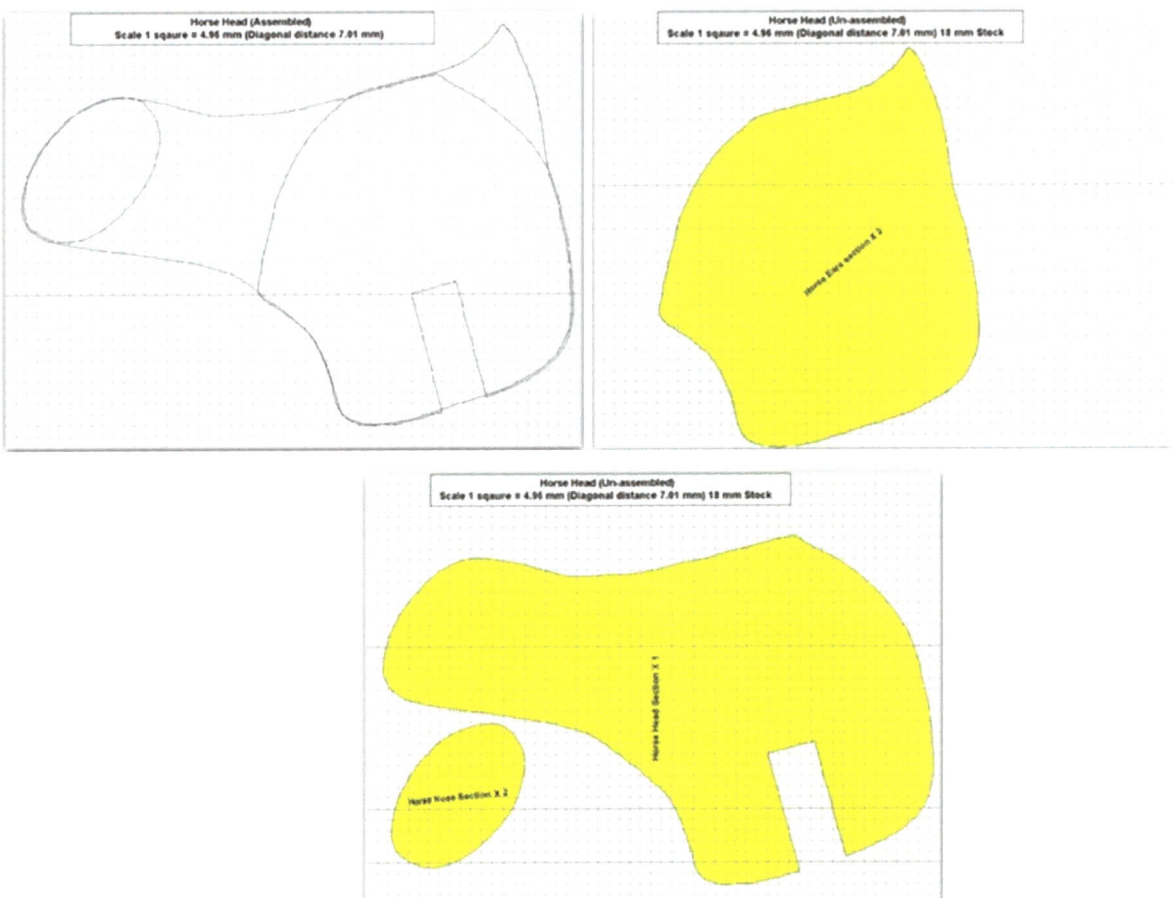

Using the Templates

The templates were laid out on the material and drawn around – the parts then being cut out on the band saw taking care to keep just outside of the lines. These were then sanded to the lines using a drum sander attached to the bench drill.

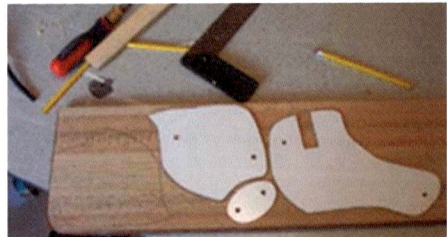

An alternative method would be to attach the templates to the material using small screws and then cut out the approximate shape using the saw and finishing of with a router fitted with a bit that could follow the attached template.

In both methods the parts would be rounded over on one side using the router and ½ inch round over bit. To keep the sections still while the rounding over took place it was placed on a rubber mesh mat (available for DIY, kitchen stores etc.) – just make sure that it does not hang out over the edge of your parts while working as the router will catch it and get tangled.

The nose sections were too small for the mat method so they were fastened to a scrap of wood, which was clamped to the bench during the operation.

Turning the Axle Case

The axle was made by turning a piece of scrap mahogany to a cylinder, the dimensions didn't have to be accurate as long as its diameter was approximately 50 mm to ensure that it would not split in use. The cylinder "axle case" was 100 mm long but could have been shorter if required – the limiting factor was the length of the drill bit available to drill the axle hole through the middle.

The case was sanded on the lathe, and then removed so that the hole could be made for the shaft of the horse using a 20 mm spade bit on the bench drill. The axle hole was then drilled again 12 mm using the centre marks from the lathe too ensure that it was centred.

A better approach would have been to drill the hole for the horse's body before turning the case on the lath and then to drill the axle hole while still on the lathe, however at the time I did not have the required tail stock bit.

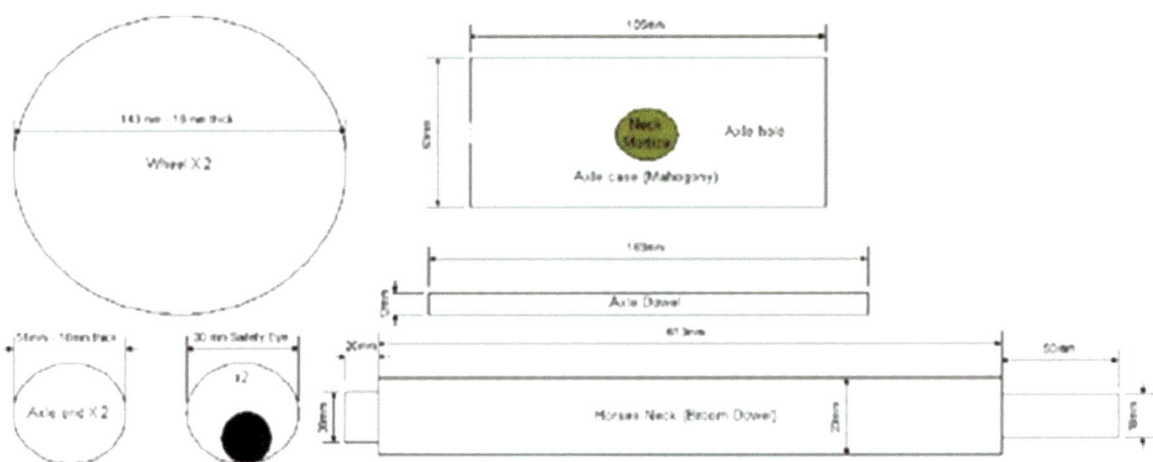

Making the Wheels

The wheels I used a CD case to draw around (approx. 143 mm diameter) and then cut out the circles on the band saw at which point I remembered that I needed centres to the circles. Luckily I had not sanded to the lines and there was just enough line left to use some geometry to mark the centres (For which I had to borrow a compass)

Start by marking an arc on the inside edge of the circle keep the compass settings the same, where the arc crosses the circle draw two more arcs (one from each intersection) to cross the first arc. Using the intersections as the centre draw two more arcs to cross each other. Draw a line from the centre of the first arc through the intersection of the last two. Repeat this 3 times around the edge of the circle and you have got the centre.

A few other ways for marking middle of a circle:

1. Second geometry method - do not cut the circles out first. Pick a point on the circumference of the circle and draw and arc inside and outside of the circle Use the point where the arc bisects the circle as the centre of another arc (don't change the compass) Draw a line through the two points of intersection for both arcs. Repeat this 3 times around the edge of the circle and you have got the centre. Use three lines because it confirms the other two.
2. Use a pin some string and a pencil - put the pin into the wood, attach one end of the string to the pint the other to the pencil at the radius for the wheel. Hold the string taught and draw the circle the pin marks the centre.
3. Turn the wheels on the lathe the middle is the point where the tailstock and active centre mark the wood..
4. Cheat use plastic wheels with a threaded bolt as the axle, this however does wear the axle case after time.

Using Dowel joints

No screws where used in this project instead dowels where employed to hold the parts of the head together. To ensure that the parts all line up drill 6 holes all the way through the main head piece and used dowel points to mark the position of the holes in the piece to be attached.

The dowels are really only to help locate and hold the parts while the glue cures so they only need to extend 4 to 5 mm into the adjoining part and by drilling through the main section only one dowel is required to hold both sides.

Gluing Up

With all of the parts smoothed off they were ready for gluing, I used Gorilla Glue for this project, It's an Isocyanate based pre-polymer so ensure that there is plenty of ventilation and that you use gloves. I would also recommend keeping asthmatics and children away while the glue is curing.

The glue cures by a chemical reaction like expanding foam and as it reacts it expands into the wood making for a very strong joint, it's also porous when sanded, which suits the finish I wanted to use.

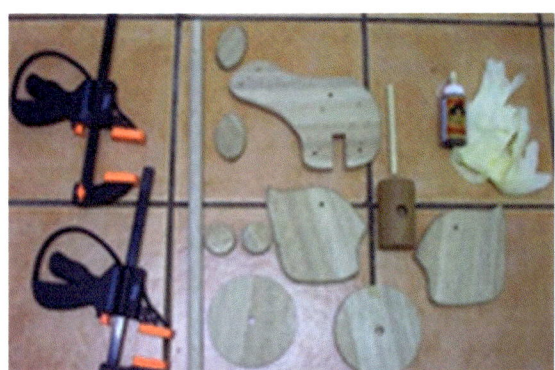

Care should be taken not to use too much glue, especially on the axle in case it spreads into areas that are needed to move, like the axle.

Axle

The axle was held together by clamping the wheel to the axle end-cap then using another clamp to hold the wheel onto the axle itself until the glue went off. Once the glue had set I applied 3 coats of linseed oil as a finish which darkened the horse quite a bit and help make it water resistant.

Head

The head was glued separate from the shaft with clamps being used to hold the parts onto the dowels until set. The eyes were simple 1 inch googly toy eyes (search for Googly eyes on E-bay and you should finds some. They have a small stud on the rear so all that is required is to drill a hole the same diameter as the stud that goes all the way through then glue the eyes in place.

Shaft (body)

The shaft is secured with glue into the hole on the axle case and then at the head end into the hole left when the cheeks are glued to the central section (see the plan picture).

These are great toys for children, just watch out for your skirting boards and wall paper as collisions do happen.

15: Trailer Trolley

If you go camping then you will probably have a trailer, ours is kept in front of the house in an area between the bay window and the external wall. When we want to use it, it has to be lifted through the gate by resting it on my knees and shuffling sideways very carefully.

Help was needed in the form of a trolley and my daughter wanted to help, so this gave a great chance to show her how to use a few hand tools.

The trolley took half a day to create and Lauren enjoyed every bit of it.

Trailer Trolley Parts list

The trolley was made with recycled materials some from work and others being the left over from other projects :-

1. Casters (4 removed from a cupboard before it went into a skip at work)
2. Nuts and bolts (various) from shelving and equipment packaging.
3. Plywood - left over from making my son a sand pit
4. Blue plastic batons - runners from a demonstration cupboard
5. Nylon cord (ex-washing line)

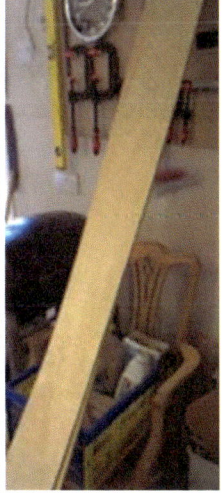

A Hobbyists Guide to Turning and DIY - Ideas for inspiration

Initial cuts

The trailer is 90 cm wide so the first parts I got Lauren to cut where the main cross beams. There would be two of everything as the plywood would not be strong enough to support the trailer in a single thickness the parts would be sandwiched together for extra strength.

8 cm was added to the length of the stretchers to allow for batons to be attached to stop the trailer sliding off of the ends. The next parts where the T pieces (4 of - remember the sandwich) each T section was 40 cm long. Once they where all cut we laid them out to see roughly how the trolley would look - see picture

Measuring for the castors

We marked the centre of the T sections and lined them up on the cross stretcher. Once centred we put a line on the T's either side of the stretcher - this gave a rectangle on either side where the castor would be fastened.

To start with Lauren found it difficult to use the saw I explained that some saws can cut in both directions, but even if it did it was easier to start with, to lift the saw off of the material between strokes - this allows you to build up a rhythm. Being the first time with a saw I did let her have a rest while I cut some of the parts.

I got Lauren to draw an 'X' (corner to corner) in each of the rectangles to mark the centre. I then positioned one of the castors on one of the 'X' marks and once happy that it was in the middle of the X I drew around the base plate and marked the position of the holes.

To mark out for the next castor Lauren squared up one of the other T sections level with the caster shape I had drawn and marked out the for the next castor relative to the fist

(no measuring needed).

Marking out for the last castors was simpler - just put the T section with the rectangles on in line with the one already marked out and use a long straight edge to mark the required positions on the new board.

Using a Drill

The T Sections where clamped to the stretchers and again a cross was marked - this time on the stretcher from corner to corner where the boards met.

I then showed Lauren how to get even spacing for the bolt holes needed to fasten the sections together. By taking one of the plastic batons which was 4 cm square and stood it at the corner of the X mark and where the opposite corner of the baton crossed the X made a mark for the hole. This was repeated for the four holes needed on the end. I then drilled the first two holes and put the initial bolts in place this made it easier to move the clamps holding the parts to drill the next two holes.

I then let Lauren drill the next couple of holes and when happy that she was working safely let her drill all of the holes fastening bolts as she went.

Bolt Up

With all of the holes drilled Lauren then attached all the bolts and fastened the nuts - I just went around then at the end to ensure they were as tight as possible.

Some short bolts

As all the bolts came from other uses (recycled) some were a little short in places so I had Lauren put a little thread adhesive on each nut to ensure that they stayed in place when we use the trolley.

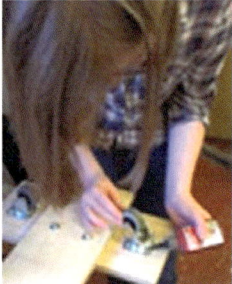
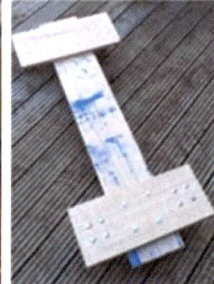

Batons and rope

Two more holes were drilled to attach the plastic batons these are very important as they provide a way of stopping the trailer from falling off of the trolley in use. The extra holes already in the batons were used to add rope pull handles to the trolley. These were made by taking some spare washing line, cut to length, and first melting the ends to prevent fraying. The line was then passed through the holes and knotted. The length of the rope pulls depends on your height. They need to be long enough to prevent you having to stoop while using the trolley.

Using the Trolley

The next day we used the trailer to go camping so we tried out the trolley - placing it so that the trailer could be tipped up onto it and sit nicely between the batons, then we just rolled it out through the gate and put the trailer down on the path outside.

 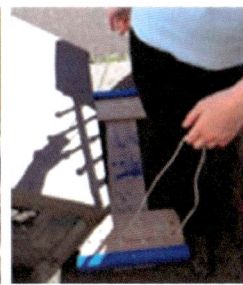 

The trolley works great and definitely makes for a lot less effort than carrying the trailer through the gate by myself and while it's not a techno gadget its one worth having.

A Hobbyists Guide to Turning and DIY - Ideas for inspiration

16: An old fashioned bogie kart

Kids bikes are becoming so cheap, and once your kids have used and abused theirs, they tend to be of very little use for another child, so what can you do with it.????

The answer is simple you buy another in exactly the same condition, strip them both down for the wheels and make a Bogie (go kart). This not only gives you fun in making it but also extra life for parts of bikes that would   otherwise be on the scrap heap.

Parts list

For this my parts list is all recycling materials (with the exception of the bolts and eyes)

1. The wheels from two frog bikes (one my sons' the other £2.00 from a car boot sale)
2. 11 cm Tongue and Groove floor boards (left over from replacing a floor cut to 60 cm lengths plus some odd pieces
3. 10 cm by 4 cm left from a garden fence - you will need 1 bit 125 cm long and two bits 55 cm long
4. Side styling - anything to hand - this is not just decoration it helps protect fingers from the wheels - I used an old living room chair we no longer needed.
5. Steel 2 pieces 50 cm by 4 cm and 5 mm thick
6. 55 cm length 4 cm by 2.5 cm scrap
7. 11 coach bolts
8. 2 eye bolts
9. length of rope

Please note that although I have given some sizes - they are not really important - if you make one of these then use your child and scale the cart from there on (add a little for growth and this is a toy that will last a long time - years not weeks)

A Hobbyists Guide to Turning and DIY - Ideas for inspiration

Axle's

Start by stripping the wheels from both bikes and remove the axles (make sure you don't lose the bearings.). Also remove any cogs from the rear wheels they will not be needed for this project.

You will be left with 4 axles clean them up and pair them - this is important as you want to have similar wheels at the front and rear. If you look at the axles and the nuts you will note that two will be thinner than the others, these are from the front wheels of the bike - I used those for the front wheels of the cart.

The axles of the cart are made by welding the bike axles to a piece of steel - now I cannot weld so for this part I took the studs to a local garage who did the welding then charged me and gave the money I handed over straight to my son (nice people).

Clamp the axle with the rear bike wheels to the first 55 cm beam and then to clamp the 125 cm beam into its notch - allow it to overhang at the rear by approximately 15 cm then drill a series of holes along its length to take the coach bolts used to hold it together.

The Chassis and steering

Take one of the 55 cm beams and make a notch in it at the half way point that is large enough to sit the long bean in, then on the other side along its length make a recess to take the steel plate of the axle, at the ends you will need to remove a little more material as the welded part of the bike studs will be facing up into the wood. (repeat this for the other 55 cm beam which will be the front axle).

Repeat this clamping and drilling process for the front axle then use a long coach bolt and two large washers to attach the front axle - for all bolts I used locking nuts , but also applied thread lock as well.

The rear needs 5 holes the front only three. on the front put the other two holes close to, but missing the weld at the wheels the use the eye bolts with large washers front and rear - this is where you will be attaching the rope

The Body

Cut some scrap T&G to pack up the space from the rear axle to the top of the long beam on both sides. and cut some extra as well, the is used to form a cross beam support for the front of the seat.

Use the scrap spacers and a length of the T&G to sandwich it over the 125 cm beam. I also used the added 4 cm bean as a strengthened under the cart.

When you are ready clamp it all together and start putting the bolts in use your children as counter weights if needed.

For the steering I had one of my children sit on the cart and hold her arms out, I then ran a length of rope from one eye on the front axle to the other while she held onto it. Then tied the rope off at a comfortable length.

This was to be the end of the cart, but I realized that the kids would at some point put their hands down to hold onto the sides with the potential to get trapped in the wheels so I used the sides from and old chair to give the cart some stylish and functional sides.

A further improvement was added once they started to use the Bogie as I found out that more often than not I was to be the motor (either pushing or pulling). This addition was a screw eye at the rear into the overhang of the 125 cm beam. I then used and old curtain pole fitted with another eye as a push rod making it easy to both push the cart as well as stop it.

About the Author

Hi my name is Kenneth Moore and this is my first attempt at writing about a hobby that I really enjoy. The contents mostly cover projects on wood turning from the point of view of an armature woodworker. It is intended, not as a strict set of instructions, but more a of showing off what I have been able to achieve in the hope that it will give others a nudge to try something for themselves. And if people copy the projects here in, then it will have done its job. Having worked in the Medical Products and Pharmaceutical industries for most of my career I have needed at outlet for the frustrations that big business can cause and DIY gives that. It's a great hobby for anyone as long as they follow some basic safety rules to protect themselves and anyone else in their working area.

I have created a growing web site (http://www.handycrafted.net). This is a site where all are welcome to visit and make suggestions and hopefully get inspiration. Please take a look and feel free to let me know what you think.

A Hobbyists Guide to Turning and DIY - Ideas for inspiration

Kenneth Moore

A Hobbyists Guide to Turning and DIY - Ideas for inspiration

Printed in Poland
by Amazon Fulfillment
Poland Sp. z o.o., Wrocław